AF428471

Ron Hequet
WINNER'S CIRCLE

'hot' topics

Marketing & Profit Book Series...Book #1

Marketing, Sales, Profit & Leadership

Motivational 'How to'...
Attract Your Ideal Customers / Clients to...
Refresh, Reenergize and Refocus Your Profit and Personal Success

Ron Hequet

Best Selling Author of...

Build Your Career 180™
Profit and Cash Flow Marketing...Fast™
The Profit Growth Calculator™
Inspirational Achievement Quotes™
Join the Winner's Circle™

Marketing & Profit
'hot' topics

PUBLISHED BY: Texas Trail, Inc.
Winners Circle™
P.O. Box 2785
Weatherford, Texas 76086

Table of Contents

Title Page--5

Copyright--6

Table of Contents--7

Testimonials---11

Sample List of Industries served-------------------12

Prologue--13

Part 1 *MARKETING*-------------------------------------14-54

Marketing Plan--55

Part 2 *SALES*---56-115

Sales Plan---116

Part 3 *PROFIT*-----------------------------------117-136

Profit Plan..137

Part 4 *LEADERSHIP*...138-195

Leadership Plan--196

Important Invitation - Decision

(So, What Do You Do from Here?)----------197-199

VIP 3% Winners Circle™

Additional Resources-------------------------------200-202

Testimonials about Ron Hequet and his Achievement Strategies

"With a history as a successful multi-business owner himself, Ron Hequet has given you, the entrepreneur, business owner, determined to grow your business, this invaluable resource."

Kevin Harrington, original 'Shark' on the hit T.V. show, Shark Tank'

"This practical, fast-moving book shows you how to continually refresh, reenergize and refocus your income and your career opportunities throughout your life."

Brian Tracy, Legendary Speaker and Author

"For any entrepreneur or business owner determined to grow their business, this invaluable resource from Ron Hequet is designed to show you how."

James Malinchak, featured on ABC's hit T.V. show 'Secret Millionaire'

"Ron, I learned what I know from you! Boom! I'm rich and it's all because of you! My hero; thanks, Ron. You are the greatest!"

Henry F. Camp, CEO, Louisville, KY

"Ron, I really appreciate what you've done to turn my business around…to lead me on a path of success and profit! Thanks…for what you do for me, my family and my business."

Ernie Dell – President, Waterford, MI

"No communication can adequately convey Ron Hequet's talents."
Henry Shallcross – President, Arlington, TX

"I am fortunate to have his personal talents for my company."
Ross Hyde – President, Fort Worth, TX

"...appreciate the value of Ron's Private Mentor Program."
Craig Thoeny – CEO, Minneapolis, MN

"Ron Hequet is a trusted source...integral part of my company."
Katherine Wilson – President, Seattle, WA

"The solutions that Ron developed and implemented...are paying off."
Gary Treater – President, West Palm Beach, FL

"Ron is a very dedicated person...Ron's work is second to none."
W. James Cox – President, Portland, OR

"Ron...I'm impressed in your mission to help others...I commend you for keeping the focus where it should be..."
Nate Woodbury – Owner, Lehi, UT

"Nothing as I expected, you are amazing...thank you for all that valuable information to our audience."
Ninon deVere DeRosa – CEO, Las Vegas, NV

"The workshop this past week with Ron Hequet was invaluable! Setting sales goals is important, but to have Ron's plan for achieving it is essential!"
John Leach – TSM, Kansas City, MO

"We reached $Xm this year, thank you Ron for helping us make it possible."
Pam Kruse, VP, Grand Rapids, MI

"I am very pleased to suggest that you engage Ron Hequet in your pursuit of excellence. Ron's workshops gave us the tools to see tangible improvements."
Tim Taylor – Executive Pastor, Willow Park, TX

"We have restructured with different and more effective cost controls, and with a pre-planned profit...I feel we will recoup 2X the investment in Ron Hequet."
Gary VanSlooten, President, West Olive, MI

"Ron provided the fuel that allows common people to attain uncommon results."
Steve Thoeny – President, Crystal, MN

"You have been a blessing to me and my business."
Kevin McKee – President, Aledo, TX

"Ron Hequet will motivate and inspire you to achieve your potential and reach the next level."

James L. Capra – Author, Leadership at the Front Line

Sample List of Industries Served:

- Aero Space Parts Supply
- Advertising, Public Relations
- Apparel Manufacturing, Distribution
- Automotive Parts and Service
- Building Trades and Construction
- Computer Assembly and Service
- Commercial Vehicle Services
- Distribution Centers and Suppliers
- Electronics Sales and Marketing
- Energy Conservation
- Engineering and Design Firms
- Food Processing Industry
- EMS Claims Processing
- Healthcare and Physician Groups
- Industrial HVAC Manufacturing
- Landscape Design and Maintenance
- Machine CNC Milling Plants
- Newspapers, Publishing, Printing
- Packaging and Distribution
- Retail, Single and Multi-location
- Technology and Software Services
- Telemarketing and Sales
- Voice / Data Products and Services

...and the list goes on...

Prologue

There are many people that have played a key role in my journey as a business owner, consultant, speaker, career coach and author of the book you have in your hands.

I am indebted to every client, for their trust over the past three decades, who sought me out and allowed me to develop and implement a business and marketing plan that assisted in making their business grow and become more profitable.

I also appreciate the long-standing working relationships I've enjoyed with my firm's associates, whose support and expertise have greatly enhanced the value delivered to our clients.

Finally, thank you to my family, who remind me that my talents are not from anything that I have done apart from God.

Congratulations…on investing in this inspirational resource.

It will affect your organization, team and individuals you associate with, whether it is customers, clients, employees or family members.

Part 1

Marketing

Make More Money...Now!

"Obstacles to your objectives should be viewed as steps to achievement."

Chances are your business lost customers in the last year and you're still waiting for the economy to turn around. Your bucket has leaks and it's likely that you don't know how many customers you lost, who you lost, why you lost them, where they went or where they are now. If you are the leader and do nothing different, I'll be able to make this same claim about your business this time next year. **Make more money now** by **not** losing customers, starting with the one you're about to lose tomorrow.

How accurately determines how much a customer is worth and how much it costs to replace that customer. This is so you can decide how much you are willing to **invest,** to **not** lose a customer. Next, decide how to split that investment into preventative versus search, rescue and recovery programs. Now create or re-create and actually **execute both** the preventative and the search, rescue and recovery programs, and simultaneously test, analyze and improve, over and over again.

Even if you have a high retention rate and urbane, multi-phased programs, it is time to test, perfect and improve it all. Your testing will reveal needed tweaks – some minor, some major and some easy and some painfully hard. No matter how long the list is, implementation should not exceed 90 days.

You should **loathe**, and I mean **loath** losing customers.

Sports teams, who win a lot, loathe losing, even more than they like winning. To be a winner, you must loathe losing. Winning is an insufficient motivator.

You **must** comprehend the true economies of losing a customer. You **must** become passionate and committed to invest uncompromisingly in not losing customers.

Getting customers is not a genius. Dotcom gets them every day with virtually no business model. Organizations that achieve do so based upon their ability to keep customers.

Are You Really Different?

'5 Branding Strategies'

Your brand identity is among your business' most valuable assets, regardless of the size of your business. It is the asset that can even increase the cash value of your business when it comes to sell your business.

But **if your business is not recognized as being different from the competition**, your brand identity does not have much value, if any. And I'm not talking about the brand names or labels of the products and services you offer; I am speaking about the brand identity of *your company.*

Branding, that is, establishing a clear but differentiating identity to your prospective customers and existing customers is imperative during a challenging economy, when no business can really afford to lose a sale.

If your brand is not different today, your brand is non-existent or you want to change your brand, the following 5 branding strategies will produce results with minimal investment.

Conduct Research: First, determine what your market's perception of your business is as it is today. Interview customers and others who know your business to get a view from the outside. Find out why they chose your business instead of a competitor and what they like most about your organization.

Next, find out if your current branding value means anything to your customers. If you **know what your customers really want and need**, you'll have an advantage in adapting your products and services directly to them and using this information for growing or updating your brand.

Analyze every aspect of your current brand, including marketing materials, business cards, on-hold messaging, email signature and website design, to ensure everything is uniform with the branding message you want to communicate.

2. **Describe Your Brand:** Write a one-page or less description of your business. Describe how you want to be different. What about your products, services or the customer experience that make you different?

    Focus on how to deliver those products or services in a memorable way.

3. **Be Consistent:** Be relentless in communicating the benefits of your brand in all marketing materials, but especially when speaking directly with a customer, because **every customer interaction is a branding opportunity**.

    This goes beyond what you may typically think of as marketing materials, i.e. product packaging (have you ever received anything in the mail from Ralph Lauren?), the appearance of your office and restrooms, staff expertise, your user-friendly website and so on.

4. **Social media:** I would never suggest that you *'bet the farm'* on social media, but I think we would all agree that it is not only a necessary part of your branding effort, but can over the long haul, find new customers and enhance customer experience with current customers.

   Create Twitter™ feeds and a Facebook™ page where you can ***re-communicate your unique value, reiterate your brand difference***, and even provide special and unique content and offers.

5. **T.O.M.A.:** *'Top of mind awareness'.* Building a brand is a process and may take months before you realize quantifiable results. It's imperative to select what areas you want to focus on first and then ***execute and stick to it***, keeping your brand 'top of mind' in your customers and future customers' minds.

   Your brand grows over time, so again, it's important not to quit and stay positive. If a customer is not ready to buy today, ***you want to be 'top of mind' for when they do***.

WIFM

'Does Your Marketing Plan Answer That Question?'

Consumers, customers, clients, etc. all seem to listen to the same station - WIFM - **'What's In It for Me?'** And I am not just referring to benefits vs. features or price. Today isn't there a desire for 'fame' or connection / belonging, even if it is at the customer level.

For instance, TJ Max has seemed to corner the Z gen market. Why? How? It used to be about 'labels. And admittedly it still is, but there seems to be a requirement for more from the consumer.

Many years ago, there was a woman who tried out for a position with the NFL; did she do so because she really thought she had a shot at making the team or, was it because she knew the resulting failure would end up being a considerable amount of publicity? Hence, opening the doors for her in other areas of 'fame'?

A serious look into social media, as well as the emulation of the Hollywood 'bad boys' (and girls), and with the current focus on 'ME', I believe, offers some **insight as to how marketing programs might be directed near term**. Could TMZ even exist if there wasn't something to this?

Even the social conscious (environmental, etc.) tie-ins seem to create an identity, **all pointed back to the individual, group, organization, etc. and not just for philanthropic reasons**.

Going forward, as always, I will be working from the office, developing business strategies and operating plans for the next fiscal year. One of the crucial components of the plan of course will be **'marketing'**, and I will be looking at how a business uses this concept to enhance their *'brand'*.

Creating a 'new school' marketing plan must answer the 'WIFM' question, and I believe its objectives go beyond just posting on social media.

Here are some key topics that will be considered in creating a marketing action plan for next year.

✓ Who is my business /customer community?

✓ How does my business maintain an ongoing positive connection with our customers?

✓ How does my business provide memorable customer experience, not customer service?

Retail Is Dead!

'Create Your Own Stage'

Sorry if that title bursts your bubble. Two of the businesses I owned were retail, and the **'good o days'** **ain't coming back!**

Retailers, **as well as many others,** need to do new and maybe extreme, to **attract new customers** and retain existing customers. *And I am certainly not referring to anything having to do with price.*

Many are faced with multiple battlefronts...

✓ Profitability in leveraging technology, internet and social media

✓ Smart phone scanning shoppers

✓ Big Box competitors

✓ Employee underperformance...and more.

For sure, marketing and advertising are imperative, but wouldn't it be **more effective and profitable** to *have prospective customers come to you, instead of you going to them*.

The average buyer sees or hears as many as 5,000 advertisements a day. You must do more to rise above the noise and set yourself apart. Retailers rely on holidays and / or vendor specials.

If your business is seasonal, you rely on a similar approach during that time.

The obvious problem...so does the competition, you're simply adding to the noise.

Creating your own on-site events sets you apart. And, when you do them during those holidays and seasonal periods, you can rise above the noise.

Create your own strategic event and **have customers come to you**. Your competition will have no opportunity to get to them or are they even aware that they are in the market for your products / services.

Your event could be big, but don't think of every event being SRO (standing room only). Your event can be used to uncover your hottest prospective customers. People who are willing to invest time in attending your event will likely be a lifetime customer.

Note: Do you know the lifetime value of one of your customers?

Prospective and existing customers are interested in education and are willing to invest time in exchange for that information. A well planned, content rich and fun event can achieve a lot. The event could be a time of engagement for existing customers and fact-finding for prospective customers.

Wouldn't it be great to have existing customers and prospective buyer's side-by-side at your event? Want to learn more? 'Call me'!

It's Not the Length of Your Pipeline

'Are You Performing Preventative Maintenance?'

We use 'pipeline' as a metaphor for the flow of prospective customers. Your pipeline doesn't have to be 'full' or you'll **run the risk of it clogging**, i.e. no time or priorities for follow up, but it does need to be populated and moving.

At the end, farthest from you are the 'undefined' leads, unsolicited or generated by you and your market gravity. These leads need to be filtered so that only suitable customers and **true** buyers remain.

As you move closer, another path provides referral business, which also needs to be filtered. Still closer you have repeat business, proactive events and calls, and even chance??

As these leads are qualified and placed in a priority setting, you should be visiting and following up, building trust and providing opportunities. At the pipeline exit, closest to you, this is actual business flow, qualified and ready to close.

You can't have 'everyone' as your prospect, and you can't treat all prospective customers the same. Decide on the ideal customer for your USP (Unique Selling Proposition).

A customer with whom you can do the things you have great passion for and are the **best** at doing.

Like the type of pipes that carry water or oil, **your pipeline requires preventive maintenance**, i.e. purging your lists, making sure customers aren't blocked by obstacles to entry and a strong flow (significant value that draws customers in the desired direction).

It's not the length of your pipeline, which ideally should be rather short, **but the growing number of entries to it...that's important**.

What Is Your Marketing Dominating Position?

'Identify and Create'

Why do your customers buy from your business instead of your competitors? If you don't know, that can mean one of two things. Either you offer a customer a unique set of advantages and benefits, but you have to date not identified them, or you offer your customer no unique advantages and **you're just fortunate to even have a business in the first place**...and there is no substance for you to keep it going.

Any time the competition wants to offer your customers an advantage you don't, **they will take that customer away from you**.

To get your customers and prospective customers to see your business as offering one-of-a-kind advantages and / or benefits that the competition does not **is the essence of a market dominating position** (MDP).

You must determine the most powerful advantage and / or benefit you can provide an existing or future customer for it to be irrational for them to choose to do business with anyone but your company. Here's how you do that.

Identify what advantages or results your customers want the most. You don't have to change your product or service, but you must position your product or service as having a unique benefit they can't get from your competitors. And **don't offer it subtly**.

Integrate your MDP in everything you say and do, in every marketing plan. When you do this, you educate your customers to know, value and want that advantage.

Remember when Avis car rental was struggling with their marketing and had no advantage. They needed a unique message. Hertz was well ahead in size and market share. Avis came up with a unique marketing position, **'We're number two. We try harder.'**

They still rented cars like Hertz, but they positioned themselves as a company that would work harder and give better service and better rates. **They made amazing progress and growth because of that MDP.**

If I said, *"When it absolutely, positively has to be there"*, what business name comes to mind? Yes, Federal Express. FedEx was the only shipping company delivering overnight. The competition wasn't even guaranteed **when** a package was delivered. FedEx offered customers a unique advantage – the package would be delivered the next morning by 10:30am, absolutely guaranteed. Period!

At the time, I thought the NBA star Dennis Rodman was a kook, but despite posting impressive rebounding numbers, he had few, if any, endorsement contracts. He created his own uniqueness – multicolored hair and shocking tattoos. With that came a fortune in publicity and product endorsements.

Now I'm not suggesting you get tattoos or color your hair, but I am strongly encouraging you to get to work on your MDP.

If you have been following me for any length of time and ever wanted to see my eyes roll, tell me your MDP is *'great customer service'??*

First, I can almost always prove you don't, but that mantra is worn out and needs to be discarded and never be brought out again.

Once you have your MDP, you can give your current and future customers a special reason to do business with you.

What do you offer?...

Make an Offer They Can't Refuse

'Marketing Discipline'

Basically, there are two types of marketing offers; **1)** a direct purchase request offer, or **2)** a lead generation offer. There are circumstances for both types, but **no marketing effort should be lacking an offer**.

On-line media provide some of the simplest direct purchase offers, i.e. **'Buy One, Get the 2nd One Free'** – used by pizza shops and window replacement companies.

I am not a fan of discounting as a tactic, but this is an offer that you are familiar with. Another common direct purchase offer, instead of or combined with discounting is **'gift with purchase'**. This offer should be linked to a hard deadline.

<u>Direct purchase offers have some disadvantages.</u>

First, they tend to forfeit price integrity and profit margin. And, being used too frequently results in training customers to respond only when there is a 'good deal'.

Secondly, the only customers that can respond are those ready, willing and able to buy right this minute, and fail to ascertain customers likely to buy soon.

Third, the offer can be easily comparison shopped, especially if the offer is online.

The lead generation offer can significantly reduce advertising waste, change a sale culture to a marketing culture, **build trust and create a customer relationship**. This type of offer is commonly used by national direct marketers like Premier Bathtubs, but rarely used by a local remodeling company.

Premier Bathtubs advertises in many media, offering a free information kit, brochures and a DVD. After someone raises their hand and signs in, the Premier has a marketing opportunity, where the local contractor would jump to offering an in-home estimate, which rarely works.

Make an offer your potential customer can't refuse.

Your offer must have a **low resistance** level. Here are some samples of **high resistance** offers.

Chiropractor - $29 Exam

Financial Advisor – Free Private Appointment

Remodeling Contractor – Free Estimate

Funeral Home – When we're needed, we'll bury you

These types of offers can be intimidating to a potential customer and require them to be in uncomfortable situations. It requires a decision almost made, but for the developing interested person, it's too big of a step forward.

The **low resistance offers are for free information sent by mail or accessed on-line**.

For example, most funeral homes advertise their name, location, years in business and a list of services. There is only an implied offer.

What about presenting a low resistance lead generation offer, like this:

Free 'Pre-Need Planning Kit' and audio CD: 19 Financial and Estate Planning Tips for Responsible Family Members', listen to our free recorded message at 000.000.0000.

The information will be sent by mail, at no cost, no obligation.

Naturally, a low resistance offer from a funeral home doesn't apply when a loved one dies suddenly or for a Chiropractor when you fall off a ladder, so you may want to think about a combination of lead generation and immediate purchase offers.

Most marketing and advertising messages suppress response by presenting only one reason to respond, requiring a customer to be 99% ready to buy now.

No one is going to the Chiropractor for the $29 exam unless they are 99% ready to deal with their back pain.

But there are a lot of people that have intermittent back pain and who would respond to a low resistance offer for information about 'True Causes and Best Ways to Relieve Back Pain...Without Surgery or Drugs'.

Diverse markets and different media will influence your decisions. Have the discipline to make your marketing dollars work harder for your business.

Make an offer they can't refuse!

Old School Marketing, You Think...It's Still No. 1

'10 Advantages of Direct mail vs. Email'

The tried-and-true form of marketing and advertising that's been around for over 100 years is still number one in *quantifiable results*.

Yes, *direct mail* is still being used aggressively and regularly by all savvy marketers. It's a crucial part of their overall marketing mix, especially when it comes to prospecting for new customers.

It has been called junk mail. But the new junk mail is all the messages you receive in your digital inbox every day.

How many emails do you delete without even bothering to open? It's common for people to delete as much as 90% of emails received without ever opening them. The average person now receives 20, 30 or more emails each day (I personally receive about 100), soliciting everything from weight loss to travel deals, from miracle drugs to the latest ramblings of so-called experts.

Yes, email marketing is an extremely effective medium for communicating and selling customers. And it is certainly more convenient and much less expensive when compared to direct mail.

However, **if you're looking for new customers,** *direct mail wins hands down*. At the back end, direct mail is cheaper when calculating the cost-per-sale.

When it comes to crafting a multimedia campaign, **it's best to use a combination** of different messaging platforms which could include email, direct mail, free standing inserts, print ads and more. Let's review how old school (direct mail) compares positively when compared to the relatively new kid on the block (email):

1. **Direct Mail Is More Reliable…Trustworthy** – According to an Epsilon study, 50% of consumers prefer direct mail to email, 67% think direct mail is more personal, 70% preferred direct mail to email when it comes to unsolicited information from unfamiliar businesses and 25% perceived direct mail offers to be more trustworthy than email.

2. **Direct Mail Can Be Three-Dimensional…Unique** – You can touch and feel it, and in some cases like scratch 'n' sniff even smell it. It has texture, visual impact, a sense of realism and validity. *Email is strictly one-dimensional*, a message appearing on your computer or smart phone.

3. **Direct Mail Projects a Personality** – The creative execution options are virtually unlimited, from different shapes and sizes to see-through windows, die cuts and intricate folds. *Direct mail enters a home through a mailbox.* Emails can be released into cyber space with a simple click of a button.

4. **Direct Mail Has Longevity** – A direct mail package can remain on a coffee table or desk for days, even weeks for future reference. When it comes to emails, they are very disposable, they are rarely kept or referred to.

. **Direct Mail Has a Higher Perceived Value** – When it comes to email prospecting campaigns, 95%+ of all emails is never opened. Direct mail will at least capture a glance. Prospects may not read every word, but there is a level of brand and offer awareness that doesn't exist with emails.

. **Direct Mail Has a Much Higher Delivery Rate** – About 95% compared to less than 50% for most email lists. Plus, *more and more ISPs like Yahoo, AOL and Gmail* are taking steps to block unsolicited emails, and this trend is expected to continue.

. **Direct Mail Provides More Details Vs. Email Content** – The life span of an email is literally seconds. A *direct mail package can hold the attention* of a prospect for a much longer period, especially if there is an interest factor.

. **Less Competition in The Mailbox Compared to Email Inbox** – Since more and more marketers are choosing to flood email in-boxes, the *competition in the mailbox has been reduced*.

. **People Are More Receptive to Direct Mail** – When it comes to prospecting for new customers, direct mail will consistently beat email, usually by a significant margin. According to a DMA (Direct Marketing Association) study, *direct mail is 10-30 times more effective* than email when it comes to generating new customers.

0.**Direct Mail Can Rely on Emotion to Illicit a Response, Vs. The Cold, Hard Facts of an Email** – An emotional tug can help marketers sell products and services.

It's much easier to touch upon someone's feelings with direct mail when compared to the one-dimensional, fact-based content of most email campaigns.

Can direct mail and email team up to bolster a marketing campaign? It's been proven time and again that **direct mail improves email response rates**.

Here's a way to combine the power of these two mediums to optimize impact. About 7-10 days before a scheduled email blast, send all recipients a *postcard* talking about an upcoming special email offer that will soon be arriving in their inbox.

This approach has been known to boost open and click-through rates. The email recipient is much more likely to keep an eye open for the soon-to-arrive email and much more likely to open and read the email, *increasing the opportunity for a sale*.

Be Uncopyable

'How to Create an Unfair Advantage over Your Competition'

*I*t's not enough for your business to be better, **you must be UNCOPYABLE**. Back in the 70's W. Edwards Deming was a consultant to Toyota in Japan. He became known for his TQM, Total Quality Management theory.

The foundation of TQM is benchmarking. With **intrinsic** benchmarking, you simply benchmark your own industry. You look at your competition, take your competitors' developments and improve on them just a little.

Every industry niche has a tactical tradition. We all copy each other. The result, ultimately nobody's different in any significant way. Studying your competition produces conformity, not innovation.

Deming created the idea of **extrinsic** benchmarking. You must study people, organizations and businesses that have no relationship to your business at all. Why would you do that?

Here's an historic example:

In the early days of Southwest Airlines, CEO Herb Kelleher knew that most airlines took 45 to 60 minutes to clean and prepare a plane for the next flight. SWA wasn't making any money when the plane was sitting on the ground. He wondered; how could he significantly reduce the downtime on the ground?

The light bulb went on for Herb after studying **NASCAR** pit crews. During the race, every second spent in the pit, refueling, changing tires etc. cost precious time on the track. Pit crews spend countless hours practicing their pit jobs to get the car back on the track as fast as possible.

Watching a NASCAR pit crew is seeing a well-oiled machine. Everyone on the team is in motion doing what needs to be done without wasting a move. In the pit your car is losing valuable track distance…every millisecond counts.

Herb Kelleher hired a NASCAR pit crew to come to Dallas and teach his teams how to make every second count. Everyone pitches in, including the pilots. As a result, **SWA planes are loaded and ready to go in about 20 minutes** and they average 10.5 flights per gate, compared to the industry average of 5.0.

Although I have owned multiple businesses, one of the reasons that I have been so effective as a business consultant is that I have never sold, manufactured or distributed the exact same products / services as my clients in over 20 different industry niches. I have the advantage to be able to ask…" **Why do you do it that way?"**

It's not uncommon for me to observe something in another industry but doesn't exist in your industry. So, I might take that something and install it in your business where it is a new thing, and it may be **UNCOPYABLE**.

11 Keys to Creating Success through Marketing Entrepreneurship

'I do not claim these as the only keys. But keys that have been of enormous benefit to me and to clients.'

1. **BUSINESS WITH SOUND ECONOMICS:** At a recent Mastermind meeting, we discussed the high costs of arrogance. Here's how it works. An entrepreneur in love with an idea is convinced that the special makeup of the idea, product and their marketing prowess will permit overcoming basically bad math.

   For instance; in a truly direct marketing business, you need no less than a 6-to-1 or greater mark-up from costs of goods and fulfillment to selling price, i.e. if it costs $10 to make and deliver, it must sell for $60+. Anything less, **your business can't grow**.

   The greatest idea and marketing cannot overcome bad math. Ensure all your economics support sustainable growth. If not, for **ANY** reason, your results will be financially upside down.

2. **POWERFUL AND COMPLETE MARKETING PLAN:** Most wealth is fueled by a reliable, effective marketing system and plan. You need **(1)** an identifiable, reachable market, **(2)** viable media, **(3)** marketing content, **(4)** and systems for attracting, organizing and maintaining a **crowd** of customers.

   The NFL, for example, thrives mostly because of TV – **without that media**…nothing…remember Arena Football?

A major marketing breakthrough to great popularity has been fantasy football games and leagues, so every spectator can be a participant.

We can analyze every successful business and find each of these parts there, and one of the 4 parts dominants. **Your marketing system must be made up of all 4 components and nothing less.** Business marketing systems made of less or fueled by something else may rise high and prosper briefly but will always fall and fail.

3. **WITHDRAWAL AND PROTECTION:** A business is a place to take money out of, not to accumulate money in or let money be trapped in.

A. Maximize your tax-deductible and tax-deferred private pension plan contributions.

B. Own the real estate your business is housed in, converting rent (an expense) to investment equity, a very different result.

If you are not consistently taking money out of your business and putting it into a safe lockbox, you are fooling yourself about wealth.

4. **LIVE BENEATH YOUR MEANS:** Many super-high-income entrepreneurs, entertainers and athletes end up dead broke while still living, by escalating their lifestyle with their income, often buying many depreciating assets and piling up debt.

The faster you get to a 'safe harbor' place, not needing earned income, the better. This ensures better decision-making.

I confess that in my early business ownership days, I made mistakes; fortunately, it was mostly cash management, of which I am now an expert.

5. INVEST IN ONLY WHAT YOU UNDERSTAND: Invest only in stocks, companies, bonds or real estate that you know and understand. I like to invest in companies. I feel I understand so well I could run them.

They have CEOs with strong marketing know-how and are driven by Marketing Systems. I have lost money twice, in which both times I was invested in the picks of the advisor and kicked myself for doing so.

Never delegate your checkbook. I sign my own checks and never let anyone else run my finances. You should want to have an intimate relationship with your money!

PURSUE LEVERAGE: Information marketing and / or franchising for example, both **leverage expertise, content and systems**.

Delivery and strategic alliances leverage **OPC** *(Other Peoples' Customers)*. You are a very serious student of your industry, including present-day and historical leaders leverage **OPE** *(Other Peoples' Experience)*.

Operating in what's called a **Success Environment**, where you are protected from distraction, leverages time and more.

This is how you and I break the Work and Money link, **by using leverage, <u>NOT DEBT</u>!**

7. **COUNT MUCH-MEASURE MUCH:** The guy on the plane who told Kenny Rogers *"Don't count your money while yer sittin" at the table, they'll be time enough for countin' when the dealin's done"*, was a dead broke hobo riding with a free ticket.

The more things in your business that can be measured, and you really do measure, the more accountability, the more known facts, the more targets are established and accounted for day by day, if not hour by hour, **the more likely you are to create prosperity!**

8. **HAVE AN EXCELLENT UNDERSTANDING OF A POSITIVE ATTITUDE ABOUT, AND A BENEFICIAL RELATIONSHIP WITH MONEY:** Prosperity is NOT just systematic, it is emotional. There is a definitive internal game in prosperity.

I have written some about these issues in all my books. After all,...I am *America's Leading Profit and Cash Flow Strategist!*

You cannot attract and maintain prosperity more than your belief system about prosperity will accept.

<u>MOST people have serious self-imposed restrictions on that belief system.</u>

9.   BE CAREFUL OF WHO'S COUNSEL YOU ACCEPT ON ALL MATTERS OF MONEY: Most folks in any particular group – the population at large, your profession, your family, have ill-advised relationships with money, have little legitimate knowledge about financial matters, but nonetheless are delighted to dispense advice.

Just because someone appears to have a large income and / or is pretentious like having a mansion, exotic cars, a yacht, a Rolex watch, etc. is absolutely zero proof that they indeed have wealth.

I have known this from over 10 years ago. I had a high income, but listened to the **'buy-and-hold'** advisors. In the end, you must keep your own counsel. Get and study the best information available, but *never surrender your autonomous authority regarding your money* to any associate, professional or media pressure.

10. DO SOME GOOD: I strongly recommend that you create a positive exchange of value with your earning of income and do some good with a predetermined percentage of that income.

It does not matter whether you subscribe to any philosophical or spiritual belief about doing well with a portion of your earnings. Like gravity, your belief or disbelief is irrelevant.

I never say that I am *'giving back'*. That implies that I have taken something. What I do say is **I am contributing!**

The world is hard-wired to reward the combination of a responsible guardian and reasoned contributions. The world will also punish irresponsibility and ungenerousness.

11. I am aware of many millionaires and multi-millionaires, as young as 30 and as old as 90. I don't know any who didn't work very hard and who still works hard.

Anyone who has wealth and claims to have avoided work is lying about one of two things; wealth or the avoidance from hard work (the exception might be the kids of movie stars and politicians).

I encourage you to find productive and profitable work you like to do. You know the adage; ***'If you love what you do, you'll never work a day in your life.'***

The reverse of this is slothfulness. *No one, no one, but no one has ever written a truthful account titled...* ***'Sloth and Grow Rich'***.

Repellant Guard Duty

'Expect and Inspect'

Recently a coaching client sent me a copy of his most past successful sales letter along with the materials sent to leads. It had been 2 years since he had inspected these lead generation marketing sales materials. During those 2 years, subordinates had taken it upon themselves to shorten it, rewrite it and change the accompanying materials, now not matching what is promised in the lead generation ads.

He said he was shocked. Are you joking? I said to him **"The fundamental truth is...don't expect what you don't inspect."**

Wandering from the proscribed way it is intended to be done can happen even in the best of companies. But in this situation, *the subordinates think they are smarter than you*. Some or all are lazy, so sending less is easier than sending more and *the continuity from every lead generation step to sale is not understood or appreciated.*

He is not alone. I have often worked with business owners who make late findings and are shocked. That's when I help them get their train cars back on track.

When I talk about marketing, profit, cash and growth, you hope for big ideas, extensive strategy statements, maybe even the magic wand. I don't apologize for disappointing you.

Let me be plain, a huge first step to profitable growth is eradicating your business of anything that is repellant to it.
A second step is inspecting every day to see if any of those repellant things have creeped back in.

Every day, every d _ _ _ day, no breach of your marketing, profit and growth fort walls should be tolerated...**none!**

More than 14.5 BILLION spam / junk emails are sent *everyday* regardless of all the efforts by server companies, platforms and government to limit them. **Click-through rates are crumpling;** MailChimp puts the high at 6 clicks per 1,000 emails. *Are you kidding – 1 million emails to get 6,000!!*

But for those who do click through according to HubSpot, 55% who visit a website, **exit within 15 seconds**. HubSpot also reports on *'banner blindness'*, pulling response rates down to fractions of 1%. Direct response marketing campaigns I've created, the response will be no less than .006%.

Still, the obituary of direct mail continues to be written. The uproar of its death combines personal use of mail, i.e. greeting cards, paying bills, etc. *which is down*, **but marketing use of direct mail is UP, UP, UP!**

Even Google is sending physical 'shock-n-awe' boxes. If you are to survive and grow and if you're against being Amazon-ed, in a highly competitive market or fighting price obliteration, you must create, master and aggressively **use direct-mail for your business!**

Prepare For Bad Times in Good Times

'Contrarian Investing'

"The time to buy is when there is blood on the streets." (Baron Rothschild, 1885) He may have been one of the first renegade entrepreneurs, a contrarian businessperson, and investor.

We all enjoy a good times economy. Neither I nor anyone else knows when the bad times will appear, but I guarantee they will. If you don't believe that, you don't know history.

When times get bad most business owners' contract and recoil but not the members of my **VIP 3% Winners Circle™**. We move forward aggressively and boldly with the knowledge that we know and continue to learn how to acquire customers and make profit. In the many years of my business ownership career, **I learned that when others zig, I needed to zag!**

I learned and now teach my clients the importance of marketing, advertising and lead generation during bad times, which is the key to coming out of those times larger, more profitable and more formidable. Increase your marketing, advertising and lead generation, don't reduce it.

My conclusion is that to beat the competition during bad times you must **double down on your marketing**, even using new media sources to drive new leads and customers to your business. Also,

double down on your sales staff, teaching them how to sell better and close more gracefully.

You will need to market all the way to close of the sale because your competition will stop.

My ownership of businesses and having experienced decades of economic cycles, I have learned that *successful companies make market share growth when they doubled on marketing and sales*.

W Clement Stone built AON Insurance during the great depression. Others that were started during bad times are IBM, Microsoft, Burger King and Disney, just to name a few.

When times are tough other business owners cower and rub their worry beads, this is the time **VIP 3% Winners Circle™** members act. This is the time to expand product lines or to invest in customer acquisition being willing to spend more to acquire the 'right' customer. Sales more to affluent customers; expand your range by adding products and services that complement what you are currently offering.

Of course, during bad times you will have to sell harder and market smarter by reading this book, **Profit & Cash Flow Marketing...Fast – *10 Ways to Outthink...Out Market...Outsell Your Competition...In Any Economy!***

During bad times it is when you can test new media, i.e. direct mail, sales letters, 3D mail, magalogs, catalogs, etc. because they will be less expensive.

You'll be able to hire great salespeople, because **they best want to work for companies that are growing and** not hunkering down. You will need to be smarter, work harder and sell longer because customer buying timelines will expand.

During bad times it is when your business needs to show up unlike any other business with *shock and awe boxes, books, special reports and massive marketing touches*, because everyone else will be competing in price.

My businesses surviving and thriving during a bad economy taught me to never sit back and take current conditions for granted.

So why am I writing about bad times? Because **now is the time to prepare**.

Get your house in order and get ready to kick butt because the unprepared will retreat. Winter is always followed by spring, but anyone who thinks winter will never come is the thinking of a fool.

Keep'm Coming Back

'Core Marketing Values on Your Customer'

If you can prevent 5% of your customer base from leaving, you can increase your net marketing and sales profit by 25 – 95%!

A *US News and World Report* study discovered that the average business loses 15% of its customers / clients / patients each year:

✓ 68% of your customers who stop buying from your business go to another because of poor or indifferent customer service.

✓ 14% leave because of an unsatisfactorily resolved dispute or complaint.

✓ 9% leave because of price.

✓ 5% go to another company because of a recommendation.

✓ 1% die.

So, **82% go elsewhere because of a customer service issue!** Unfortunately, most customers who leave don't bother to complain...they just leave and don't come back.

It's been proven over and over that getting new customers is one of the most expensive things you can do to grow your business. Once you get a new customer, you simply cannot afford to lose them.

Every business category is facing more and more competition every year. Just about all categories have a version of a national chain, discount franchises and the internet, making it harder for you to thrive. **But this is great news for you!**

At a small business conference where I was one of the presenters, I asked the audience of 250 people in attendance if they had a product or service that customers couldn't get anywhere else. In the entire room, only two hands went up, and I'm confident their competition believes there is an alternative.

Practically no one has a unique product or service that people can't get elsewhere. You must give your customers a reason with your company rather than your competitors. The number one area that will give you the highest return for your efforts and money is providing the best customer service.

And **I'm not talking about customer service in a box and the canned** *'Thanks for shopping at ABC Company, have a nice day'* type of customer service.

I'm talking about **customer service with your core values**, where even if you mess up, your customers will come back because they believe in you and your team and are not just satisfied but loyal and tell others about your business.

Black Friday Sales

'Losing Its Luster?'

The reports are in...*Black Friday sales began in October*, way before American shoppers even began to think about Thanksgiving.

In the weeks leading up to Thanksgiving, retailers have pushed out nonstop **'Holiday Deals'** and **'Early Access'** promotions intended to get customers to spend early and often. *However, many shoppers now view Black Friday as just another day of **stuff on sale!***

When these customers do buy, more are doing so online. I read a report that stated for the first time, most U.S. consumers said they will do the bulk of their holiday shopping on their computer and / or mobile device. The persistent question seems to be, **is this the best deal I can get, or maybe I should wait another two weeks?'** Retailers are offering more deals and starting earlier, but *consumers aren't excited!*

Is Black Friday now bad for business? The reality is that Thanksgiving weekend has become a time when retailers treat their worst customers like royalty. Many retail strategies and tactics fail to realize that not all customers have equal worth.

There are high-value customers who have an ongoing relationship with a retailer and make highly profitable purchases throughout the year. Then there are low-value customers, **the type that Black Friday attracts**.

These customers have almost no relationship with or loyalty to a retailer and only occasionally make purchases. And those purchases usually have low margins.

On Black Friday, retailers tend to overly invest in low-value customers, pulling out all the stops in the hopes that doing so will somehow turn them into high-value customers...
wrong...never happen!

How to Build Trust

'Never take this process for granted!'

People naturally seek safety and security. You and I need trust. Without trust, it would be nearly impossible to love, nurture friendships or conduct much business. You and I crave trust and when we really *feel* that with a business or person, it's a connection that is very hard to break.

Step 1: *Define and locate your target market!*

I ask new clients who is their target market, and the response is usually, 'Everyone is'. That is true for no one. Identify those who can **buy** and the **willingness to buy**, via demographics, psychographics, et. al.

Step 2: *Get your ideal customer's attention!*

You must pop up on their radar many times (with more than email). Once you've connected, you need to **get a small commitment**. Depending on your products / services, this could be a *small sale, an appointment, consultation call* or other similar step. **Provide the opportunity to get to know you, like you and trust you!**

Step 3: *Connect and relate!*

Depending on the level of commitment you received in Step 2 i.e., getting an email address is low, all their contact information is mild, asking for information is good, making a small purchase is excellent. ***Don't expect it or hope it will happen by itself!***

Marketing Plan

Part 2

Sales

Happy Customers - Increased Sales

'Implement A Continuous Process Improvement Program'

If, your business does not have a program executed to capture what your customers are saying, then you are missing one of the fastest ways to enhance sales and profitability. How do you know what's working or not working in your business? What processes are you analyzing and implementing to make it easier for your customers to do business with you?

Every day, depending on the size of your business, there are many opportunities to improve your 'customer's experience'. I can't tell you the hundreds of times I have heard over the years from business owners, "we have great customer service". It makes no difference what you think, what does the customer think? What does your customer 'really' think?

No highfalutin technology is required to start an improvement program. Every time you or one of your team members has a customer encounter, listen' to what and how they are saying it. There is increased sales and profit opportunities coming from their mouth.

Write down and file what they say in 3 folders: green for compliments, red for concerns and yellow for suggestions.

✓ I just received your _________, and it really helped me with _______...
(compliment)

✓ It really bothers me when I call and _______________… (concern)

✓ I wish you would ____________… (suggestion)

These are just simple examples, but I would suggest that you write down what customers are saying immediately after the encounter and worry about classification later.

At the end of the week or reasonable period create a report and analyze it with your team leaders. Do this consistently and don't stop. This valuable data will now be used to develop and execute changes for improvement. Some of the benefits to your customer experience will be…

1. Uncover the core issue your customers are experiencing and then solve that problem.
2. Eliminate pointless steps in your business processes, saving time and money.
3. Praise and recognize team members for the collection of this valuable information.
4. More…

I have seen happy employees and dissatisfied customers, but never unhappy employees and happy customers.

"If you know the combination to the achievement lock, it has to open."

Sales Staff...Gotta Believe

"Change in behavior cannot take place without a change in belief."

Think about it, anyone who doesn't 100% first believe in themselves, and then also 100% believe in the product or service their selling...how can that person achieve?

When my daughter was in grade school, she used to play with Zig Ziglar's granddaughter who lived nearby. Zig used to say, "Timid salespeople have skinny kids". Now, neither he nor I is advocating being overweight, but I think you get the point.

Even if you believe in yourself and the product or service you're selling, but not demonstrating that belief to others through the basics of the sales process, i.e. prospecting, qualifying, presenting and closing...then it's going to be tough making sales.

After selling my last business to consult full-time and doing speaking and seminars, I have always, while helping others, conveyed with confidence my personal knowledge and skillsets.

Why or how, because I believe in myself and in my ability to help others. If you are in sales or have any responsibility for sales production, get a sales staff line-up who believes.

The Sherlock Holmes Tactic for Increasing Sales

"Some of the best opportunities and subsequent achievements go to those who have an affinity, not for working hard or smart, but for working 'right'." ©

There are many ways for your organization to maximize opportunities that gain another customer and / or increase revenue. In my business I always wanted to execute every tactic I could, not wanting all my marketing or sales tactical eggs in one basket, so to speak. We have all heard that 'information is power', or **'success leaves clues**. Well then, why not *put on your Sherlock Holmes hat and investigate your way of increasing sales*?

If you are not currently communicating with customers by phone, **DO IT NOW!** Yes, you need a reason. But there are many reasons for contacting a customer by phone, but one of the first and most logical is a follow-up call post purchase (this tactic also applies to any business that has inbound calls).

How? This is where the Sherlock Holmes tactic comes into play. Ask customers open ended, **investigative type** questions. These questions must be scripted, prepared in advance. Don't attempt to 'assume'.

And I recommend that you get team members' input. Since they are **on the case,** they will think of questions that lead to **'clues'** you may overlook. Next, be prepared to write the customers' response down as they speak.

In just a matter of days you will have obtained **'clues'** to increasing sales, customer relationships, buyer loyalty, marketing data and so on, all being key insight to your market.

I have asked a few sample questions to **start** your Sherlock Holmes investigation.

B2C

1. How would you rate your experience with our company?
2. Why did you choose the product / model / make etc. that you did?
3. Is there something else (product add-on / service) you would have purchased if we offered it?

B2B

1. What's going on that's exciting at your company or what are the major initiatives?
2. What is your biggest challenge currently?
3. What new products are being introduced in your market?

Once the **'evidence'** is compiled and analyzed by Sherlock (you), and your sales team, the organization will be able to strategically develop and implement tactics, processes and procedures that will **'close the case'**.

However, don't put your magnifying glass away. This must be a never-ending investigation, never allowing for a **'cold case'** to increase sales.

Low Wage Earners Does Not Equal Low Expectations

"Change in behavior cannot take place without a change in belief". ©

Have you ever been taken to task by someone who said that you shouldn't be critical of poor job performance of low-level, hourly wage earners (oh my, that includes lawyers), and various menial jobholders because *'They can't help it.'*

These critics are bigoted and condescending. Just because a person is not earning a lot of money, doesn't mean they're inferior **or that I should expect less of them**.

I expect the girl at the drive-up coffee window or the guy throwing a burger my way to be **intelligent, personable, and competent**. I assume they possess these traits or how else could they hold down the job or pass the interview? (Politics aside, I laughed when people accused former President Trump of being 'stupid'. He built skyscrapers and multiple real-estate projects all over the world, how stupid can you be to do that?)

Employers should expect their staff to have and use basic competence and people skills **in any job, at any level**. A highly paid surgeon who is arrogant and rude is not to be excused for those traits, despite their skills with a scalpel. A person who cleans your house for $20 an hour is to be respected and dealt with civilly, politely, and professionally.

I have met quite a few rich, nasty people and would not want to hang with them, and I have met many poor people who are a pleasure to be around, and who perform their work with pride and dignity.

So, aside from **stupid management, who can put things in the way of any worker in any capacity**, front-line people are not 'bottom of the barrel, and to expect less is prejudice.

On the other hand, when that person is impolite, does not know the basics of the job or shows no initiative and concern, I blame them for their behavior, which **should have been uncovered before they got the job**. That has to do with character not W2 forms.

So, when taken to task over your job performance expectations of low wage earners and when they are simply not competent, or it's stipulated that the very aspect of being a low wage earner is reason to excuse the assumed incompetence, then *that isn't just the pot calling the kettle black.*

How to Motivate Sales Staff in Any Economy

It's Not Money, its Preparation!

Most organizations are not changing the way they motivate sales teams, although they should and almost aways want to, but don't think they can or know how.

Here is an outline of how I have successfully motivated salespeople and what I would do today.

1) **Look of Success:** Psychologists have proven that if we think we look like a winner it is reflected in our behavior and everyone who meets us senses this same winning aura. Regardless of your industry, stop looking and acting like the competition. You may allow for a casual look, but jeans and a shirt that look like it was just pulled from the hamper is not business casual. Neither is putting your hair up in a clip as you run out the door to work.

I believe in individuality, but creating a 'team appearance' can add to a winning look for anyone who has face contact with customers. For one of my companies that had an outside sales staff, I brought in a personal image expert (at my expense), and paid for clothing, makeup, hair, etc. That 'Hollywood Celebrity bad boy / girl, I don't care because I'm famous look' doesn't work for top performing salespeople.

2) **Sales Managers Sell:** Today, Sales Managers who do not perform the same job as the people they manage do not have the same office cred as those who do. It is almost impossible to really know what it is like out there from behind a desk. Consider providing the manager an assistant, if necessary, to make his management time more efficient and to free up time to sell.

) **Train and Prepare:** Particularly in uncertain times, training costs should not be cut. The harder the times, the more important training is. The success or failure of 90% of all sales interaction is determined prior to the first contact.

<u>There is a powerful aphorism that goes something like this:</u>

The owner, when questioning the amount of money, the consultant wanted to spend on sales training, said "What if we spend all this money, train people, and they leave?" The consultant calmly looked at the owner and said, "What if you don't spend this money on training, and they stay?"

) **Over-communication**: Contact every past, present and future customer and key vendors. Act with enthusiasm, by having engaging, positive contact. Your company will either get more business now or be first in mind when the customer pulls the trigger.

There is no question that financial reward is a key factor for achievement, whether it is in sales or any other function that contributes to the Profit and Cash of the organization. However, in my experience, money alone will not assure success. But when you combine preparation with rewards for achievement, you will have a significant edge over the competition.

8 Steps to a Positive Sales Presentation

'Lessons in the customer experience'

Even when you make a persuasive presentation, many times it takes weeks or months of follow-up before you get a decision. Therefore, the objective is to burn memorable and positive examples with key points into the prospective customer's mind.

Still, what does the average sales presentation look and sound like?

"Hello, I am John Jones. Please allow me to introduce you to the team: Dick, Steve, and Susan. Thank you for your time.
We are from the XYZ Company...This is what we do...This is how long we have been in business...This is what we are known for...These are our customers you may know...We would like you to be our customer too..."

Is that boring or what? 'Who gives a hoot'? This is a sales presentation offering a ho-hum first impression. So, what's a more positive and effective technique? Model these eight steps and create one that fits your business and is **focused on the customer experience**:

1) **Genuine Tribute:** Begin with something that your prospective customer or their company is proud of.
This demonstrates that you've done your homework, i.e.
'Congratulations on the success of your recent product launch, marketing campaign and expansion.

2) Outline Their Challenge: *Do not talk about your product or solution.* A more positive approach is to speak to their current problems, challenges, or opportunities, i.e. *'We believe this is the right time to make a bold forward move and...'*

3) Positioning: Now is the time to present your positive solution / product or service. Afterwards, everybody else thanks the prospective customer for their time...***so don't***.

Instead; *'We appreciate the opportunity to discuss how our company's solution, products or services (be specific with your recap) can help you overcome your problem, challenge or seize this opportunity.'*

4) Recognize and Thank Your Champion: If you have an advocate inside that prospective customer's team, now is the right time to thank them, i.e. *Thank you, Jennifer, for your generosity of time and information that helped us understand your company's problems, challenges or opportunities.'*

5) Provide Experience and Testimonials: Your prospective customer must understand how your product or service will **'profitably' improve their business**. Your success stories, case histories and testimonials are powerful tools, do fail to use them.

You are now presenting yourself and your team, not as just another salesperson, but rather a trusted advisor with a consultative selling approach.

6) Review the Key Points: As a rhetorical question or make a simple statement based on your premise, i.e. *'So how will your company be better by doing business with us? Or "As you heard, the way our company would approach helping you overcome your problem, challenges or seize these opportunities is...'*

7) Close with Confidence Not a Question: One mistake many salespeople or sales teams make is to close with a closing question. Do you think your prospective customer hasn't heard all the closing questions? **So, don't!**

Close on a positive height and then **let your last words linger**. It depends on the intricacy of your offering or how many people are involved, but you may want to say something like... *'At this point, the next step that makes the most sense is...'*

8) Highlight Your Key Point / Benefit: Your last words are perhaps the most important, so **never bring up another new idea** you have no time to develop. It'll sound like you're scrambling.

Instead consider something like this; *'Again, thank you for the opportunity to demonstrate how our approach, solutions, products or services is what you want to achieve success with your problem, challenge or opportunity. We look forward to our next meeting.*

Mr. Prospect, remember the results of [testimonial of another successful customer]. They brought us in with the same timeline as yours. So, you have the benefit of knowing we pioneered this solution, etc.

Most salespeople are reasonably persuasive in the heart of their presentation because of their preparatory focus on their offering. But very few know how to open and close effectively, being positive and memorable.

And by positive I don't mean all smiley faced and all that typically accompanies an overexcited salesperson, but the positiveness that comes from the perception of being confident.

If I called you right now and asked, *How are you going to open and close next week's sales presentation?*

Your spontaneous response should be exactly what you will say and how you will say it. **Are you prepared?**

Is It Your Customer's Job to Remember You?

'A Secret for Being Memorable and Get More Business'

No, it is not your customer / client's job to remember you. It is your responsibility to be memorable. **Here is a great tactic to add to your being memorable.**

Don't email, I don't know about you, but I have enough of my time sucked away with yet another email… **'delete'**. 'Call'? Yes, call your five best customers; those who you want to use as testimonials.

Even if it goes to voicemail, say…"*Tom, I never get tired of telling the story about how – I, my company, my staff, etc. (fill in whatever is appropriate) provided the product / service you wanted. Would you mind telling me in your words about your experience with me, my company, our product / service (again, fill in whatever is appropriate)? Did we reach or exceed your expectations? Did the value meet or exceed the product / service? With your permission I'd like to get a phone appointment to make note of your comments, or at least send you a response card with a self-addressed stamped envelope. I would like to use your responses as part of my customer testimonials. Let me know when we can talk.*"

Your **happy customers will not object to this contact**. In fact, they will most likely be flattered to be asked and personally featured in your testimonials. And you'll be surprised at how convincing they are with their endorsement. They'll be complimentary and offer better phrases or rave reviews than you can imagine.

In your sales presentations and posted testimonials **you will have the actual words** of what they have said about you, your company, staff, product / service. If possible, get a photo of the customer. You'll be able to post a real face with the testimonial, and we all like to see our own picture.

Don't be reluctant to call. The very fact that you are calling **will often remind them they need more of your product / services**. Or maybe they were talking about you to a friend, and they now have a referral for you. This has happened many times in my business over the years, even if I just called to reconnect. I've also experienced it from the customer side, when one of my vendors called me.

There is an unwritten rule that when you contact a past or current customer; you must have a reason…**and it better not be that something is on 'sale'.**

Calling to ask for a testimonial is a great reason to call. Even if your customer declines (which is extremely rare), they remain flattered that you asked and **make you memorable**.

At the same time, you update and keep your testimonials current and set up an opportunity for ongoing business…just by picking up the phone, **you'll be remembered!**

Great Customer Service? Really?

'How You Communicate Is the Key'

Everyone would like to boast as to their business having great customer service. In fact, when I performed a *'business analyses* of a client's operations or even asked a business owner in a casual conversation... *"What makes their business better than the competition"*, **I almost always hear** "We've got great customer service"; to which my usual response is, **"Really? How would the customer know that?"**

This claim is almost always unsupported by definitions of exactly what constitutes 'great customer service' or as **I prefer to call it, the 'customer experience'**. How would your business determine that your service or the experience is, in fact, worth what you charge for your products / services? On balance, if your prices aren't commensurate with truly great customer service and wonderful experience for the customer, then what's the point?

I've always tried to teach clients that it is a *'great customer experience'* **when it is perceived by the customer**. There is no other area of service that adversely affects customers more than the way you communicate. So, let's put ourselves in the customer's shoes. The following is just some of the defining points to consider.

1. **Response time:** Would your customer receive a return call from you, at a minimum the same day. Ideally, you'd return calls within a few minutes. Email responses would always occur within 24 hours.

2. **Deadlines honored:** Data, reports, information and anything else requested by a customer would be delivered at worst on deadline as promised and in best case, considerably before the deadline promise.

   This includes last-minute requests. If you've agreed to a deadline, then **do it as promised** so your customer never has to follow up with you. Customers hate it when you say, I'll call back at 1 o'clock and it's now 4:00 and they haven't heard from you. Call at 1:00 even if there's nothing to report.

3. **Am I a priority:** Unless you're working with another customer, you always take my call. If you already know I'm a dissatisfied customer, you don't use caller ID to 'screen the call'. I never feel rushed, taken for granted or patronized. If my call has to be returned, I expect that when we do connect, **I will not be competing for your focus**, I have your undivided attention.

4. **Support functions are qualified and professional:** Nothing beats the phone answered by a live person, **nothing!** And, if any part of an employee's job function is to be on the phone, why would you place a person in that position whose American English diction and language understanding is difficult for the caller?

   Broken English is different face-to-face vs. over the phone, especially with VOIP and cell phones. However, if customers speak with your assistant, answering service, or even voice mail, are they treated with respect and don't have to **'jump through hoops' in your voice mail hell**. Your assistant never puts me on hold and doesn't mispronounce my name. Also, customers don't want to listen to the same commercial for your company every time they call just to leave *you* a message.

5. **I perceive trust and transparency:** You don't add to my problems, and you truthfully inform me in advance, when something has gone wrong. I don't want to ever sense that there are turf battles within your organization that affect me, your customer.

6. **You provide value:** Your website, social media, newsletters, mailers, etc. offer informative articles, tips, ideas, references, and other resources which are non-promotional and clearly helpful.

7. **You exceed expectations:** You provide more than I anticipated before and after the sale and your intent is clearly to ensure that my *'customer experience'* cannot be equaled by a competitor.

A great *'customer experience'* is a wonderful differentiator. It requires no capital investment and is often easier for a small company to deliver than it is for a larger, more bureaucratic or public organization to maintain.

Assess your customer service and *'customer experience'* with the sample **No.7** I've offered above. Additionally, it is imperative to be able to **define, articulate, train and enforce this culture**, and then deliver it to every customer's communication experience.

Great customer-perceived service *always* **contributes to the perception of value**, so they'll need to be manifest from the first point of customer contact.

Do You Support Sales?

'Three Must Haves'

*A*lthough the function may go by different names, i.e. producer, rainmaker, account representative, salesperson, **there is no more valuable function in any organization** than the individual or team that completes a sale for products and services.

Sales assistants, automated sales programs, or enhanced customer service can be helpful support tools to any sales organization. But based on my experience, there are three critical but foundational issues that must be in place to **support an effective sales team**. After all, and to state the obvious, without sales there is no *'Raison d'Etre'*.

1. **All Employees Sell:** Everyone from the warehouse crew to the bookkeeper must philosophically believe that they are in sales. *Most employees do not understand or appreciate how the jobs they perform contribute to or take away from sales efforts and customer retention and / or growth.*

2. **Sales Managers Sell:** Today, Sales Managers who do not perform the same job as the people they manage do not have the same credibility as those who do. It is tough to really know what it is like out there **from behind a desk**.

Consider providing the manager with an assistant, to make his or her management time more efficient and to free up time to sell.

3. **Train and Prepare:** Particularly in hard times, training costs should not be cut. **The harder the times, the more important training is.**

The success or failure of 90% of all sales calls / contact with a customer is determined prior to the first contact. Experience is not a substitute for pre-contact planning.

Winners always pre-plan. Winners can spend as much as 3 hours planning for a 15-minute sales call. Rehearsing from 2days to 2weeks is not uncommon for ***Winners!***

Landing the Big One

'How to Prepare for Knocking on the Door'

One of the businesses that I owned / operated during my career was a very small, apparel design and production company. I knew that if I was going to turn this little firm around and grow the business significantly, **I was going to have to land a large customer** or two while maintaining the existing customer base.

There was simply too much time and effort required to grow sales from more customers like the current customer profile.

I believed *'Landing the Big One'* could be done, because the designs were fashion forward, all handmade in the U.S., utilizing the new micro-fibers, French stitching and a high price point, worthy to be sold by certain big ones.

I also knew that we were a small niche design and would appeal to certain large customers, because of our exclusivity.

After I selected the big but special customers that would be my focus *(Hilton Head, Disney World, Nordstrom's, etc.)*.

I next had to educate myself on how large companies function and discover the best approach to selling to them.

Here is a summary of the steps I followed to *'Land the Big One'*.

Adapted your product / service and industry to the following:

1. **Build a customer contact list:** I had to probe and build a list of specific people (Decision Makers, not buyers) within the purchasing departments. I had to **be willing** to make many phone calls. I had to **be resourceful and persistent**.

2. **Develop an introductory package:** I created a cover letter, stating our **points of difference,** and a sample current customer list. And since I was targeting only a handful of 'big ones', I could afford to enclose swatches and designer renderings.

3. **First call:** 2-3 days after the package was received by the customer, I called but had to do some digging to find out if my materials were seen by the **'*Decision Maker'*** or someone with influence (just because it's addressed to the DM, doesn't mean they will see it – especially at a large company).

4. **Second mailing:** Now I'm working to offer this customer detailed information about my company, financial stability, production wherewithal, testimonials confirming margins and sell-through and a sample of a finished item within the line.

5. **Make a date:** 2 days after the detailed mailing arrived, I called to set up a presentation of the full line. **I didn't ask if they wanted to meet,** I assumed and just asked for a date, and almost always got it.

6. **Teaser mail:** For those customers who stalled in setting a firm date for viewing the line, I sent another mailing 2 weeks after the last phone call, enclosing different designer renderings, possibly a preview of next season's line.

7. **Last call:** Naturally, I followed up by phone a few days later to **'make a date'** for a presentation. It was rare for me at this point to not succeed in getting the date.

Many small or mid-sized business owners and sales executives are fearful of trying to land the big one.

I have implemented and executed this same strategy and tactics with clients in many different industries. It can be done and it's easier than you might think. However, **you must be willing to do the homework, put in the time, and be patient and doggedly persistent** to *LAND THE BIG ONE*.

Do Your Sales Teams Practice?

'Lessons from the Football Practice Squad'

One of my favorite movies is the inspirational story of **Rudy Ruettiger**. The 5' nothing young man who wanted to play football for Notre Dame? You know the story, he eventually achieved enrollment at Norte Dame but could only qualify for the football team's **'Practice Squad'**.

At least on the college and pro level, football teams have starters, various position players and a *'Practice Squad'*. Each week the starter's line-up against the practice squad to gain experience in dealing with what a real opposing team may do during a real game. The objective of course is to improve their odds of winning / achieving success.

Your sales manager should implement this same strategy. **Most of all sales training is woefully deficient** in *'real world'* sales simulation. [Every time I board a plane, I hope the pilot has had sufficient time in a flight simulator]. Your sales leaders must ensure their team is prepared, not only for each sales presentation, but for unforeseen circumstances that might occur during a real game / sales process.

In my own previous businesses and with client's sales teams, the best way I've found to create a *'practice squad'* type of environment is **"role play"**. Just like the football practice squad drill, I video-taped the play.

It was a *'yellow flag'* when a trainee would say to me, *"I can't do it with you, Mr. Hequet, but I can do it with a customer"*. No, if you can't do it with me, in a friendly, not for real simulation, then you don't get to practice on a real customer / real game.

During the role play, whoever played the customer's part was given a script to act out. The script was based on real-life customer interactions. The one-on-one situation is easy, and I know you understand my brief set-up. But what about a *sales team* 'practice squad'?

Sales Team Practice Squad Training Drill:

Multiple salespeople work together on a practice squad project and compete against other members of your sales team. Below is an example of a practice squad drill, to ensure salespeople understand your sales structure and the sales tools available at your company.

Elements of the practice squad drill:

1. A detailed description of your organization and its go-to-market strategy and tactics
2. A description of 4 to 7 potential players / actors (employees of your company), titles, etc.
3. An overview of the industry your company competes in
4. Limited financial goals
5. Miscellaneous data / information

The Drill:

The salesperson or team makes two sales calls. The first call is with one employee of the simulated customer / company, and the second call is with two other employees of the simulated company.

Each call is 10 to 15 minutes long. The competing team members used pre-call planning tools and a set of sales discovery worksheets to summarize findings.

Note: The individuals who played the roles of the customer had their own scripts that included additional facts, i.e. inside political issues, personality styles, and hidden agendas.

The Play-Back:

A formal presentation by the sales team that included:

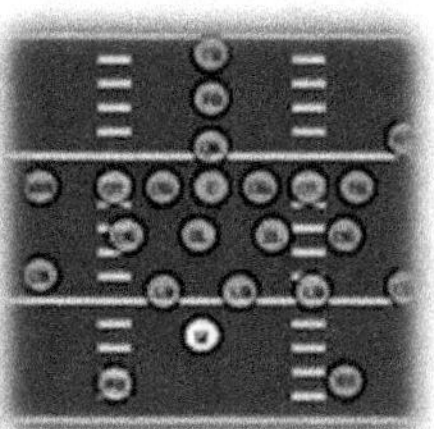

1. What they exposed during the encounter

2. Insights of the customer

3. Potential product / service recommendations, including a sales presentation that makes the case for why the customer should buy.

Implementing the '**Practice Squad**' type of training, your sales leaders can view their salespeople in action, observe their skills, and test their determination.

Depending on the size and scope of your organization, you may have to tweak these drills, but regardless, I am a believer in the effectiveness and results of role playing.

Placing them in pressure situations as part of their training, **like the football practice squad,** will improve their performance, **like the star players on the field**.

5 Attributes of Great Salespeople

'How to Hire the Same Sales Achiever Every Time'

As promised, I'm going to deliver on describing the process that I used with my own companies and with client companies to discover excellent salespeople.

The precise hiring process is different for every organization, but the procedure to develop the process is the same. However, I believe these 5 attributes will play a huge part in your organization's sales success.

First, I created a spreadsheet to score each attribute X's the weight of importance of the attribute. A perfect score is 10 for each attribute and the weight range is from 1 to 9, not 1 through 5 (need help with creating this score card, call me).

Teachable Heart: The capacity to take in and apply coaching. Having a teachable heart has been a very weighty factor in my hiring choices. After all, you can teach content, but you can't teach enthusiasm or the willingness to learn. Here is how I might assess this candidate attribute.

Step 1: Conduct a role-playing situation that parallels your customers.

Step 2: After the role-play is finished, ask them to self-evaluate their performance. Their response gives you your first perception of their teachability.

If they say, "I did great." **_Red Flag!_** You hope to hear thoughtful consideration of what was good and what could be improved.

Step 3: Offer one point of positive reaction and one point of constructive improvement. Now teach the candidate how to improve in that one area, while closely observing whether they are detached or taking notes and asking questions.

Step 4: Redo the role-play and ask them to apply some of your teaching. Don't look for perfection, look for effort.

You have just invested a few minutes in this person and if you've observed significant improvement; think about what strides could be made in a very short period.

Inquisitiveness: The skill to understand a customer via questions and listening. You and I were all taught to 'qualify' a customer. Usually, the customer felt they were being led, instead of sensing that you were sincerely interested. Great salespeople establish trust and really want to understand the customer's objectives, wants, desires, fears, etc. all via focused questions and conversation.

Step 1: First impressions still count. When you greet the candidate, do they ask you a question, i.e. how's your day, or based on their research by your company, do they reference what they observed, and do they follow up with another question?

Step 2: Conduct a role-playing situation that parallels your customers.

Prior Achievements: A verifiable background of notable achievement. This is most likely the easiest attribute for you to assess.

Look for a historical rank in the top 10% among their previous sales team. If they are not coming from sales, class rank in school, a sports team star, team captain or a leader in an organization, competitive drive?

Intellect: The knack to learn multifaceted concepts and explain it in a clear way. If you sell a commodity, this attribute is not as weighty as maybe work ethic. But if your company sells a product or service that is evolving, intellect can be a significant attribute.

Step 1: Right from the first phone interview, expose the candidate to new industry information and see if they have the knack to understand and relay it back to you.

Step 2: Send the candidate some of your training materials and ask if they learn the materials prior to the next interview.

Attempt to recognize two things; how well did they understood the concepts and how well did they explain what they learned.

Work Ethic: Proactively producing results of the organizations goals with enthusiasm. This can be the most difficult attribute for you to assess. Here are 3 tactics you can use to assess a candidate's work ethic.

Step 1: Pay attention during all interviews. How fast did they return your phone calls? How quickly did they return deliverables, i.e. resume, transcripts, references, etc. Did they drive the interview, or did you have to pull them in?

Step 2: References: Don't ask, "Did they work hard?" Instead say, "Rank this person according to teachability, inquisitiveness, intellect and work ethic."

Step 3: Remember, you can teach content, but you can never teach enthusiasm.

Every organization's customer environment will require a special sales hiring method. However, I have found that establishing hiring criteria according to these 5 attributes will consistently prove to provide your organization with the same sales achiever every time.

How to Bond in a Sales Presentation

'Trying to Sell Something...Big Mistake!'

Regardless of your industry niche, the products or services you sell, most salespeople make the big mistake of kicking off a sales presentation by trying to sell something.

Big mistake...there is no bond with the customer, who wants to buy, but does not want to be sold.

Once you truly understand and accept that **people don't like to be sold, but they like to buy**, you will at once change the dynamics of your sales presentation.

If you want to bond and engage with your customer, the conversation must be about **them**, in terms of **them**, proving value and profit for **them**.

If you do not achieve a bond with your customer, the buyer will ask for a proposal, stall, offer some objection, say they're just looking or any of the usual ways of escape.

The first sale that must be made is...you. A bond must be created by making it all about **them**. *If your customer does not buy you as a person, they won't buy what you're selling.*

That Little 'Sweet Spot' In Your Customer's Head

'Are you doing anything to set your business apart?'

I's it possible that the growth of on-line sales is because of the deplorable **'customer experience'** you encounter when you go shopping?

When I go into a business, I almost always know exactly what I am looking for and want to buy. But after I have a chance to look around and can't find it, and without someone noticing me or asking if I need assistance, I can't help but wonder how they stay in business (and maybe not for long).

Yes, I understand that women are more prone to 'looking around' (shopping), with no intent on buying that day. **But can you risk that?**

When I can't find what I'm looking for by myself, now I must search for someone to help me. They often make me feel like an interruption to their day. I usually leave and chalk it up to their apathy; to them it's just a JOB.

As once a multi-business owner myself and a business consultant, you know what also drives me crazy. When a business serves me, but **they do it just like everybody else**.

When you go to the store and make a decent sized purchase (I don't mean a trunk full of groceries), what happens next? I'll tell you. 99% of the time the answer is nothing.

You can buy a television, computer, a suit, or anything else you so desire and 99% of the time they let you walk out without thinking twice, or if you're lucky, you may get a half-hearted "thank you please come again."

So, you can imagine how a friend of mine felt when he got a **thank you note** in the mail at his home from a high-end shoe store, about 3 days after he bought a pair of shoes. I'll tell you how he felt. He told me that he couldn't wait to go back and buy another pair of shoes (he did)!

You see, some sharp salesperson thought about the fact that sending a simple 3 or 4 line thank you note was **enough to make that salesperson stand out in a crowd**, over the hundreds of other salespeople he's bought products from in the past.

Even though it was a very small gesture, it surprised him so much that he now looks forward to buying shoes from this store. He now has a mental **'sweet spot'** when he thinks about that store and brand of shoes!

How much would your business be willing to pay to have this little **'sweet spot'** *in your customer's head?* Do you think your business could have it for a 47-cent stamp and a couple of handwritten lines?

Is your business **just like all the rest**? Are you doing anything to set your business apart? If not, you should be!

Customer or Client?

'How to Understand Their True Wants and Needs'

Customer: *A person who purchases a commodity or service*

Client: *A person who is under the protection of another*

If your business uses the term customer, fine, but always think of and treat them as clients. And when you and everyone in your business have this mindset and begin to 'serve' clients instead of selling clients, you will **out-perform the competition**.

What exactly is "under the protection of another"? It means you don't 'sell' a customer the product or service just so you can make the highest one-time margin. **You must understand and value precisely what they want and more importantly what they need,** even if they are unable to verbalize the exact desired result. [I know, this is sales 'qualifying' 101 but done with the goal of protecting the client with care]

Once you know the ultimate result or outcome they want and need and you lead them to that outcome, you become a trusted adviser who protects them, and you've given them reason to remain a lifetime client.

Example: When a father comes into your bike store with his 6-year-old to buy his first bicycle, what is he looking for? What does dad want? Does he just need a bicycle?

No, **dad wants a life-long memory, a shared
experience**…teaching his son how to ride a bike, just like his dad
taught him.

Dad wants that once-in-a-lifetime experience when his son, speeding
down the street, shouts, "Look Dad, I'm riding a two-wheeler."

So, do you sell dad the top-of-the-line, with the highest margin?
Maybe, if that is the best solution. But consider telling the father that
you've sold hundreds of first-time bikes, and you know what a
wonderful memory he and his son are about to have, but possibly a
less expensive model might be better. It's his son's first bike and he
may crash it into a tree. You've made the sale and just became a
trusted advisor to the father.

Dad recognizes **you didn't just sell him, you 'protected' him**.
He's now a client. In a couple of years, his son will need a new bike;
where do you think dad will go to buy it? And maybe the entire
family will want to ride together.

When the time comes for the son to buy his little boy or girl their
first bike, where do you think they'll go?

Examine your business. Do you focus on giving value and advice,
understanding a prospective client's true wants and needs, instead of
'selling'? If so, you and your business will be profitably rewarded.

What Would I Do If I Lost It All?

'What would I do first?'

"I would get a sales job, and I would start working". Success is almost impossible, in any field, without solid sales skills.

Here's why. To many people, the word selling implies manipulating, pressuring, cajoling, all the used-car-salesman stereotypes.

But if you think of selling as explaining the logic and benefits of a decision, then everyone, business owner or not, needs sales skills: to convince others that an idea makes sense, to show bosses or investors how a project or business will generate a return, to help employees understand the benefits of a new process, etc.

In essence, sales skills are communication skills. Communication skills are critical in any business or career, and you'll learn more about communication by working in sales than you will anywhere else.

Gaining sales skills will help you win financing, bring in investors, line up distribution deals, land customers; in the early stages of starting a company, everything involves sales.

Understanding the sales process, and how to build long-term customer relationships, is incredibly important regardless of the industry or career you choose.

Spending time in a direct sales role is an investment that will pay dividends forever.

<u>Here are a few of the benefits:</u>

1. **You'll learn to negotiate** – Every job involves negotiating with customers, with vendors and suppliers, even with employees. Salespeople learn to listen, evaluate variables, identify key drivers, overcome objections, and find ways to reach agreement, without burning bridges.

2. *You'll learn to close.* Asking for what you want is difficult for a lot of people. Closing a sale is part art, part science. Getting others to agree with you and follow your direction is also part art and part science. If you want to lead people, you must be able to close. Great salespeople know how to close.

Great bosses do, too.

3. **You'll learn persistence** – Salespeople hear the word 'no' all the time. Over time you'll start to see no as a challenge, not a rejection. And you'll figure out what to do next.

4. **You'll learn self-discipline** – When you work for a big company, you can sometimes sleepwalk your way through a day and still get paid. When you work on commission, your credo is, *"If it is to be, it's up to me."* Working in sales is a great way to permanently connect the mental dots between performance and reward.

5. **You'll gain self-confidence** – Working in sales is the perfect cure for shyness. You'll learn to step forward with confidence, especially under duress or in a crisis.

Still not convinced. Think of it this way: The more intimidating or scary a position in sales sounds, the more you need to take one. You'll gain confidence and self-assurance, and the skills you gain will serve you well for the rest of your business, and personal life.

So, if you're a would-be entrepreneur, set aside your business plan and work in sales for a year or two. If you're a struggling entrepreneur, take a part-time sales job. Part of the reason you're struggling is probably because of poor sales skills.

Knowing what my sales skills are and the products that I can sell, I think I could find a job selling a product that had enough commissions or rewards for me.

And that would generate enough money to let me start my own business and let me use my sales skills to make money for myself, not for an employer.

Successful business owners, successful people in general, spend much of their time 'selling'. Learn how to sell. It's the best investment you will ever make.

5 Keys to Sales Success

'Goal Setting...Write It Down!'

Here's my fundamental keys for you to achieve all of your sales goals, and it's simple. It's very important to break your sales goals down to the activities necessary to achieve them.

Please understand you can't control the sales themselves because sales can go sideways for a thousand reasons, but you can control the activities which yield or lead inevitably to those sales by the law of probabilities. So, the more precise you are about these activities, the more likely you will accomplish your sales and your income goals.

Here's the procedure for you to complete breaking down your sales goals into the precise activities you must do to achieve each one of them. **BTW: If it's not in writing...it's not real!**

1. **Start with your sales volume, and your income goals.**

✓ How much do you want to sell? **Write it down!**
✓ How many sales will you have to make to achieve your income goals? **Write it down!**
✓ Work out what you earn per sale and divide that into your earnings goal. **Write it down!**

For example, if you want to make $50,000 this year, at $500 per sale you'll have to make 100 sales.

2. Calculate the number of contacts you'll have to make. **Write it down!**

- ✓ You may have to contact roughly 15 before you make a sale. **Make a list!**
- ✓ Therefore, you'll have to make 1,500 calls.
- ✓ Now here's an important point: **keep track** (crm or whatever), of your call activity every day so that you can measure how well you're doing.

3. How many presentations will you need to make to close 100 sales?

- ✓ Maybe you'll have to make 3 presentations to make one sale.
- ✓ That means you need to make 300 presentations for 100 sales.
- ✓ **Write it down!**

4. What about the number of proposals?

- ✓ 1 of these prospects out of 3 buys, so the other 2 need proposals; so, you need 200 proposals.

5. Daily activities: How many customers will I have to call every day to achieve my goals daily, weekly, and monthly? **Write it down!**

If you break it down and **write it down**, as I've instructed, then the first thing you do on Monday morning at eight o'clock is for you to start working on your numbers. **Your job is to accomplish your numbers.** If you attain your numbers every single day, as sure as the sun rises in the East, you're going to hit your numbers every week and every month.

You'll have high weeks and low weeks, and high months and low months, but on average overall, you'll hit your targeted goals again and again.

The big mistake many make is when you don't make your numbers on Monday, Tuesday or Wednesday, and then you really pour it on Thursday and Friday. But on Friday, you work a couple of hours and then quit saying, *"I'll work on it twice as hard next week."*

And you get further and further behind. The key to success in sales, since you're on your own so much of the time, is to **hold your own feet to the fire**.

Case Study: A good salesman with my client company in Minnesota asked me to personally coach him and provide a system of my sales *'Action Guide'* discipline.

After some one-on-one time with me, I learned about his learning style, i.e. visual, auditory, or kinesthetic. His learning style was kinesthetic. So, after he arrived at work, I would prevent him from having a cup of coffee (and he really liked coffee), until he had made 5 sales calls. Next, we wouldn't go to lunch until he had scheduled 2 appointments or made 5 more sales calls.

You may consider this self-disciplining. But he told me that *'when you start missing lunch and feeling that hunger because you procrastinated and fooled around all morning, and you keep your promise to yourself, you'll get smart really fast.'*

He said, "*You stop fooling around*". You get in there in the morning, and you realize that lunch is at stake...so you make the calls. As a **'personal affirmation'**, say to yourself...
'My lunch is at stake. I'm here to talk to you.'

Always break down your goals into the activities necessary to achieve them. Once you're aware of what needs to be done... **you'll have no excuse not to do it**.

Thank Goodness for Objections

'How to Prepare and Respond to Sales Objection'

Before I started my first business I was one of twenty seven salespeople with a distribution company. Like most newbies, I studied, attended workshops and role played with others. **The secret** I learned was that the better I got at preparing and responding to customers' objections, the higher my closing percentage.

During my entire tenure with that distribution company, I was always either number one or two each month. If I wasn't number one, it was Bill G. It was a friendly competition.

In my first two small businesses I was the lead salesperson. So, my sales closing ability was directly tied to survival. The key...**welcome objections**, because they are necessary.

Prospective customers, in the deepest recesses of their mind still think of the car salesman. They want to feel that they have made a purchase and not been 'railroaded' or 'smooth-talked' into something. The customer usually presents it as objections instead of questions.

You must **be prepared** to respond to objections both in face-to-face presentations and in print. **Yes, in print.** Your prospective customers are asking these same questions at home or office about your product / service offering.

7 Common objections and how to prepare and respond:

- **PRICE:** Explain or demonstrate quality, superiority, service. Break down the price, i.e. $360, is only $1 a day. Your competition may be cheaper, but what about quality / service and detailing any differences in the products.

- **I CAN'T AFFORD IT:** Explain the terms and use the 'selling money at a discount' scenario.

- **PRODUCT IS TOO NEW:** Show test results, testimonials, newness is progress, your company has not spent a lot on promotion but instead invested in research, development and improvement.

- **RUMOR:** I've heard, such n' such. Explain why it's unfounded. If somebody had an actual issue, explain what was done to correct the issue. If it's a complaint from someone they know, they offer to speak with them and go about correcting the problem.

- **PERSONAL CONNECTION:** I've done business with them for a long time; they're like family, etc. Offer a test scenario to assist in breaking the tie. Demonstrate product / service superiority. Attempt to gain a portion of the business, and then give them good reasons to switch totally.

- **I HAVE TO TALK IT OVER:** Typically, this refers to a spouse. Schedule a joint meeting ASAP. Call the spouse right then and get approval or appointment day and time.

7. <u>**WHAT WE HAVE IS STILL GOOD:**</u> Focus on new features and benefits that make the other old hat. Demonstrate increased production, efficiency, savings, reduced maintenance costs, etc.

Anyone in sales, regardless of industry niche, product or service, who doesn't welcome objections, is foolish.

Objections are the keys to closing the sale.

Contact Us...Not!

'5 Actions to Ensure Customer Loyalty'

Whether you call it 'Customer Service', 'Customer Care' or 'Customer Support', almost all of my research obtained by calling numerous companies service phone was a very disappointing experience.

First, why would anyone place a person in the position of customer service on the phone, when their American English **diction** is not their first language?

I could tell many of my calls were answered by what sounded like south of the border or the middle east. Now I don't go there, I am not bias. **We are talking about handling your customers' issues, placing orders, handling returns and most of all having the knowledge and authority to answer customer questions.**

It was our turn to host this past Thanksgiving at our home. Because of my client travelling at the time and since our kids and grandkids live hours away and would not arrive until about noon, e.g. no help, we decided to order the holiday feast from the famous...
<u>*'Harry & David'*</u>.

'Harry & David' offered a complete turkey dinner with all the *fixn's*. However, the number of pounds of the turkey was not posted.

So, I called to find out. After going through their phone menu, push 1 for…push 2 for…, etc. and waiting for my call to be answered…finally a person answered and like a bad **diction** machine gun – I *think* they stated their name and asked how they could help me. I asked a question; how many pounds the turkey is.

I swear I didn't understand a single word. I asked again and besides not understanding what they said the phone connection was breaking up, plus I could hear all the other agents talking in the background…the acoustics of a gymnasium…I hung up.

I called a second time, with the same results. I called a third time and finally got a decent connection and although his English **diction** was not great, I could at least understand him. How many pounds is the turkey? He said, **"I don't know"**. I asked him how we could find out. I was put on hold and after more than a couple of minutes he had the answer.

What a terrible experience from a company that is supposed to be high-end.

Also, have you noticed that many on-line companies do not post phone numbers? Customer service… (NOT), is via email.

A Facebook ad from a company named MackWeldon.com caught my attention because I was in the market for quality sweatpants. It was $78 plus S&H. I was a little concerned about the size but selected and placed my order.

When I received the product, the fitness wasn't perfect. I went to their website and guess what? No phone number, only email. I sent an email requesting a quick phone call and provided my contact number.

Two days later, the following is what I received in response to my email.

Your request (1234567) has been received and is being reviewed by our support staff. Please allow 3-4 days for a response. Please rest assured that your email is important to us, we will read every word and respond with as complete a resolution as possible. Any delays in our response will not impact on the return policy.

This email was sent to me in February. I had yet to hear from them. **They lost me as a customer forever.**

If I asked you who is most important, you or the customer, you would all probably say...the customer. But **you don't speak it or act it**.

Your customer service says...

- ✓ The person who handles that is on vacation this week.
- ✓ That item is out of stock, and I don't know when we'll get more.
- ✓ I'm sorry, that's the best we can do.
- ✓ That's not my department.
- ✓ I don't know how you got it before...but this is the way we do it now.
- ✓ [digital voice] Your call will be answered in the order it was received.
- ✓ I'm either on my phone or away from my desk.
- ✓ Our policy is...

Customers don't give a flip about your policies. Businesses distance themselves from customers with auto-attendant; press 1, press 2...

Customers call, contact or walk through the door for one reason...**they need help!**

How to ensure customer loyalty:

1. The person who signed your paycheck did not put the money there, *your customer did*.
2. Positive attitude is the determining factor of your ability to serve. I read 'The Power of Positive Thinking', by Norman Vincent Peale. **Deliver positive words and actions** *before your competitor does!*
3. The lifetime value of a customer is 20 times their annual purchases. **Service action or educational communication** (not email), is just as critical for long term loyalty as a sales action.
4. Customer **satisfaction is no longer the standard measurement** for assuring repeat business. Ask your 10 best repeat customers why they stick with you, to learn what makes them loyal.
5. Don't ask an ad agency; word-of-mouth promotion is way more powerful. We all ask others where to shop, where to eat, where to live and so on.

What's the word on the street about your business?

Great customer service is mostly a 'feeling' that we may not necessarily be able put into words, but **we know when it's bad or good**. Bad; call the DMV, or any government agency, any national retail or restaurant chain. Good; L.L. Bean, Hobby Lobby or Lamps Plus. *Which feeling does your business communicate?*

Finding Your Distinct Advantage

The *Harvard Business Review* long ago reported that if you can prevent 5% of your customers from leaving, you will increase your net profit by 25% to 95%.

A *U.S. News and World Report* study found that the average American business **loses 15% of its customer base each year**.

68% stop buying from one and go to another because of poor or indifferent service,
14% leave because of a poorly resolved dispute of complaint, craziness
9% leave because of price,
5% go to another based upon a recommendation, and
1% die.

Therefore, 82% go to another business because of a customer service issue! And so it is within your power to cut off 82% of your business' loss of customers. I want to tell you that it has been my experience that **very few business owners invest enough in this**.

It's sad that most customers who leave don't bother to complain. And then you spend a lot of time, money and resources to get new customers to replace those who left.

Competition is everywhere, on-line and off-line. You probably can't be 'THE Low Price Leader'.

If you're a retailer, you can't beat Walmart. If you're in menswear, can you beat Jos. A. Bank's 'Buy One Suit, Get Two Free, craziness? What about to the homeowner or B2B, can you beat Amazon's assortment? You'll find the answer inside your business…it is called customer sales service.

At an event where I was speaking, **I asked the audience of approximately 500 if they had a product or service that couldn't be purchased anywhere other than their business**. Only two hands went up. The other 498 knew they had no unique product / service advantage. *That's a good thing to confess, because then you can act accordingly to find and develop a different advantage.*

Practically no one has such a unique product / service that customers can't get anywhere else. So, you need to give them a reason, and **the primary area where you have the greatest control, and where you can get the greatest return for your efforts and money is Customer Experience.**

What I'm talking about is not the canned, "Thanks for shopping at Jumbo Mart, have a nice day" type of customer service!

When I was hired to do a Seminar about customer service training, I ask this question: What *should* you be doing when it comes to the 'customer experience'?

1. We tell our staff to deliver good customer service. *They should know what that means.*

2. We tell our staff to deliver good customer service; give some examples, but nothing formal.

3. We have meetings about customer service *occasionally* and tell everyone they should give good customer service.

4. All new staff get customer service training *when they are hired.*

5. Everyone has gone through our customer service training, and they are consistently and persistently reminded about our customer service expectations. Good results are acknowledged. Problems are discussed. Statistical measurements of retention and referrals are communicated.

Almost all hands are raised to number 5. But if you press for the truth, they embarrassedly confess that it's some variation of 1-4. They defend the contradiction by saying they are too busy or can't get good employees.

With the best of intentions, you have a *'rah-rah'* meeting about customer service and the service improves for a few weeks. Without a formal on-going training program things go back to the way they were *'before'*, every time.

More than 75% of all business owners have no upfront customer service training for new employees – NONE! So, what should you do? And don't take any of this for granted.

✓ Train your entire team to deliver your distinct 'Customer Experience.

✓ Constantly reinforce your customer experience expectation with your team.

Nido Qubein says: "Motivation without foundation leads only to frustration."

Zig Ziglar says: "Repetition is mother of all learning."

Ron Hequet says: "Regardless of job title / function, no one can be allowed to be part of the team without receiving customer experience training!" Make it number one on your goal list –

Find your distinct advantage.

Over Deliver

'How to Sell at Premium Prices and Profits'

What I want to share with you here is that this is not just a marketing exercise. To command premium prices, you have to **target customers who want premium experience**. You must upgrade your game...and just raising the bar in your business with your deliverables is not enough.

You not only need smart marketing and advertising, but you need to make the experience your customer has a **premium experience**. If at any time in your process it triggers a customer **'UH-OH'**, these folks might be ordinary, (e.g. just as crappy as everybody else) can ruin everything.

As an example: Owners of a multi 7 figure, affluent aimed practice has smartly invested in getting and adopting top-level scripts and processes for the handling of incoming calls from prospective patients, obtained from a client.

But these calls are being handled by whichever front desk person is available to take a call.

Their business is large enough to afford having one person dedicated to nothing but these inbound calls and making follow-up calls – a person good at it, focused only on that and in a separate office set up for that important job.

All calls are turned over to this person, which will improve the experience your customer has with the initial conversation / experience.

This is 'marketing sales' in the same way **RAY KROC** defined *'always clean restrooms'* as a McDonald's *marketing expense*, not operations. It was more about the customer experience and before they even made a purchase.

Your attitudes, thinking and your commitment to over deliver in the customer experience, while protecting premium sales prices and profits will wind up ruling your business success.

The best strategy and tactics for selling at premium prices and profits is **upgrading your game**. That's a good thing for your customers and for you!

Only Happy Customers Return

What best describes your *'customer service training'* in your business?

. You tell your staff to deliver good customer service. They should know what that means.

. You tell your staff to deliver good customer service and give some examples sometimes, but nothing formal.

. You have meetings about customer service occasionally and tell everyone they should give good customer service.

. All new staff get customer service training when they are hired.

. Everyone has gone through my customer service training, and they are consistently and persistently reminded about our customer service expectations.

Over the years, in my customer service seminars only about 2% answer no. 5. Here's what happens in most businesses. With the best of intentions, you have a **'rah-rah'** meeting about customer service and the service improves for a month or so and then you're back to where you started.

Ongoing training doesn't happen because you're a busy business owner and have lots of other things to do.

Over **75% of all businesses have no upfront consistent customer service training** for new hires. _What to do?_

First, train your entire team to deliver exceptional customer service.

Next, consistently and persistently reinforce your customer service expectations with your team.

Start with the 'rah-rah' training I mentioned, but it can't stop there. Consistently and persistently reinforce those expectations.

Zig Ziglar said, _"Repetition is the mother of all learning."_ At the end of the day, what you really want is **behavioral change**.

Now that you have your entire team trained and are consistently reminding them of your customer service expectations, you need to ensure that every new team member gets the exact same initial training.

Oh...*Him* Again

I am blessed not to have this problem, but you may know of someone who does. You know...the friend or family member that is referred to as **'that guy'**.

He's the guy where, anytime you see his number on the caller ID, you know he is calling to hit you up for a favor or for a loan. No matter how many times you dodge him, he somehow finds you.

And no matter how bad you want to end the relationship, you don't because he's a friend or family. He acts like he's your friend, but only when it's a friend in need.

The average small business only communicates with its customers when it wants or needs something. You may act friendly, yet you only appear when you are ready to ask for something.

- Buy my new product or service.
- Can you give me a referral?
- Will you write a good review for me?
- Here's my ad with what's on sale.
- Can I have your email address so I can send you promotions?
- Give me your cell phone number, I will text your coupons.

Does it remind you of someone? Many business owners are **'that guy'** to their customers. They *see* your email, advertising, hear your voice and say to themselves...'**Oh *Him* Again!**

Sales Plan

Part 3

Profit

Tactics for Constructing Benefits

"If you know the combination to the profit achievement lock, it has to open."

*I*f you retain nothing else about sales presentations or promoting your profitable organization, remember this motto, *'features tell, benefits sell'*. Here's a few of the top examples...*(dated, but still apply)*

Feature: 6 CD Changer

Benefit: 7 hours of continuous audio without the frustration of changing CD's while driving!

Feature: Our company offers a seminar on job search.

Benefit: You'll learn the 7 steps you must take to land that dream job in today's economy!

Feature: You'll get a DVD set featuring John Smith, a business profit expert.

Benefit: In module 2 you'll learn the insider secrets to managing your business from your Balance Sheet, creating great cash flow and operating profit.

You'll agree for certain...**features are boring**. So, stop using them! Begin using benefits that show your prospective customer what your products / services will do for them. **Translate for the prospect** by finishing this sentence...'Here's what this means to you', e.g. 'It has a 6 CD changer...and here's what this means to you...' *Got it?*

Why are benefits imperative? Easy...people care more about themselves than they care about you or your company.

Are they wrong? No matter, it's just a fact of life. You must convince your prospect that your product / service will help them solve their problem or fulfill a desire. I have witnessed salespeople saying something like this, "My product is awesome because it does this and it's designed to do this and oh, it can also do this". This is all about the product and not the prospect.

When properly constructed **a benefit should be about what will happen** in the life of the prospect when they buy your product / service. If not, the prospect may not buy, and you run the risk of turning the prospect experience with you into buying a commodity.

An example is the old standby that goes something like this, '*We've been in business since 1994*', or '*We've got great customer service*'. What's wrong with that? Everything!

First, nobody cares how long you've been in business and the quality of customer service is customer perceived, not from your business staff. So, how do you take those standard lines and make it a benefit for the customer?

How about saying, "*Because we've been in business since 1994, you can be assured that you will always receive fast and dependable service. There have been a lot of drycleaners [your business] coming and go in this area, but we're still here. And we are here because we put our customers first and that means when you trust us with your clothes [your service] you're getting almost 30+ years of quality and service*".

Do you **see the difference**?

Now what if you are a brand-new business? How can you use being new as a benefit?

"The reason we're the right cleaners [your business] for you is because we use the latest technologically advanced equipment guaranteed to clean your shirts, dresses and suits perfectly [your service]. Others may have been here longer but they're still using equipment from the 70's; systems that have been proven to cause damage to clothes and reduce their life. Our systems are not only clean but restore your clothes to that 'off-the-rack' appearance".

Now, take the time to re-write your sales presentations to indicate clearly the benefits of your product or service, **as perceived by the customer**.

Just imagine you're speaking with a customer and filling in the blanks.

"Here's what this means to you________________."

Do You Have Customer Loyalty?

'How to Drive Profits with Great Customer Experience'

Customer loyalty is an obvious link to **profitability**. Not only with my own previous business but also having consulted clients in over 20 different industries, I can confirm that happy customers, happy for having done business with your company are **much more likely to be repeat customers**.

But making a customer happy is only one of the many issues that determine real loyalty. They range from...the number of accessible competitors, available information about those competitors and how difficult or easy it is to switch to a different company...all have an impact on loyalty.

So, before you decide on the importance of customer satisfaction as compared to loyalty, it's important to think about the other influential issues.

Even if you somewhat dominate your market with your products / services, dissatisfied, unhappy customers will work to find a way to do business with companies who aren't even known for great customer experience.

You may remember when Direct TV started. Their business grew because customers were unhappy with their cable companies that treated them poorly, and did so because they thought customers had no option.

Your customers, who have repeatedly great experience, hand over more of their money and are more loyal to your business. Research I've done indicates that **customers are willing to pay a premium** to a business known for high levels of customer satisfaction, especially if that is confirmed with their personal experience of doing business with you.

And, great customer experience is often relayed to others, encouraging others to do business with you. Regrettably the inverse is true as well, only with more force. Unhappy customers are much more vocal and willing to share their unhappy experience with your company.

Therefore, test that you have everything necessary to ensure a **'customer perceived'** great experience, and if so, it will significantly contribute to customer loyalty and a growing profit bottom line.

Do You Have So Much Vision, You're Blind?

'We Never Heard That'

If the average person reacted to losing cash with the same calm as business owners do when there is a drop in their equity, there would be a lot of folks observing the family farm being auctioned off.

I have seen businesses having created all sorts of vision statements and mission statements which caused them to lose sight of what should be an uncomplicated goal: **to show a profit!** They have so much *'vision'* that they're blind.

With all the planning tools, strategic mediums, industry reports and conferences, business owners often don't have any idea as to what they're doing strategically.

As it was for me in the beginning of my business ownership career (despite all my degrees), there is typically nothing in the route to entrepreneurship which prepares you to be a strategist, nor would most recognize an applicable strategy if they tripped over it.

Do you remember IBM, Sears or Braniff? And that's just some of the 'big boys', who are supposed to be in the know.

Many years ago, I attempted to work with the board of directors of a resort operation in Ohio that was not showing a profit. The board had a debate as to which comes first: *strategy, objectives or goals*.

As I tried to explain that the terms were not important (even though they can have the same meaning),
but creating a **Profit Plan** for the future of the business was imperative.

I then put them through the task of determining what their tactical strengths were and what forces powered the business. **The 12 people in the room individually came up with about 20 different points and / or combinations,** which didn't surprise me.

This demonstrated that the top team had never discussed and agreed on the key factors that powered the business and were making decisions that were often contradictory.

The CEO glanced at me with that, *I told you so'* look on his face. The CEO addressed the room and expressed his disappointment in them not knowing what was obvious to him and what he had communicated in the past. **Unanimously, they all fired back, we never heard that'.**

It may have been clear to the CEO, but it had never been **communicated and confirmed** with the leadership. And like an old-fashioned Sunday afternoon drive; the business went casually down the road.

The afternoon session that was supposed to be dedicated to objective decision making was canceled. **Oh, did I forget to tell you;** *all the 12 board members were related families.*

The Right Way to Plan for Customer Loyalty

'Myths and Reality'

No doubt it is possible to be profitable, at least in the short term, by focusing on lowering expenses and at the same time disregarding creating an excellent customer experience.

Even if you are sold on creating a strategy for providing great customer experience, you may still be unprofitable if your strategy is founded on the naïve dependence on one or more of the old customer loyalty myths.

My current knowledge has progressed to the point of having found flaws in old traditional beliefs. Don't dismiss customer loyalty as an achievable strategy. There are customer loyalty realities associated with profitable organizations that are proof to the right way to plan the great customer experience.

Here are 7 realities to creating a customer loyalty strategy:

. **Don't manage customer retention before you manage customer selection.**

. **Customer loyalty requires more time to develop than you are currently willing to give;** planning and patience are prerequisites.

. **Focus on your customers' share of their purchasing power.** Don't neglect customers because of your current low share; learn to increase your share of their loyalty.

4. **Loyalty must be mutually beneficial.**
    Are your efforts skewed in your company's favor?

5. **The course of actions leading to profitable loyalty can be complex.**
    Analyze the response patterns of your customers that lead to loyalty.

6. **Happy and loyal employees will make a difference.**
    I've never seen unhappy team members with happy customers.

7. **Great customer experience and loyalty are not without a great brand image.**
    All your marketing plans, sales programs, communication, policies and procedures must be linked and mutually promote and confirm your company's brand image.

Customer loyalty is not dead. Sadly, neither are poorly managed customer experience and loyalty plans. You operate in probably the most competitive environment ever.

I for one would rather do business consistently with the same vendor, retailer, etc. But show me inconsistency or only a pretense of good service and I will take my money elsewhere.

Creating a great customer experience and loyalty strategy along with its tactical plan of execution is not an option. Your planned dollar investment in this strategy will return profitable rewards now and in the future.

Perceived Value Must Always Exceed the Cost

'3 Basic Influencers'

How does your prospective customer perceive your offer? Is there a sense of urgency; will they buy from you now or decide to 'think about it'?

In the latter case, your customer probably perceives your offer as an expense rather than an investment.

Perceived value must always exceed the cost or your product / service. It's been said, *if you can't put a price on your value, then all you can price is your cost'*.

There are 3 basic influences to perceived value:

1. **Economic Value:** This is the financial impact of the investment. What will the ROI be like? What will it financially do for my team, my department or my company? Will it reduce operating costs, improve inventory turnover, and improve cash flow?

   These are questions on the mind of the economic buyer, who makes decisions exclusively on financial considerations.

2. **Organizational Value:** What can this investment do for the business; increase productivity and efficiencies? This is the question in the mind of the user(s).

3. **Personal Value:** Not always quantifiable, but nonetheless it's real in the perception of the user. What will this investment do for me personally; increase my sales; help me get a bonus or promotion?

Personal value is as equally important as the economic and business perceived value but is often the determining influence in your customer's decision, which can only be exposed when there is trust and a good rapport with the decision maker.

Your customers buy / invest when the value received is perceived as exceeding the dollar cost.

How do your customers perceive what you offer?

6 Profit Growth Tactics

'Plug the Holes in Your Profit Bucket'

*I*n my many years as a business consultant / coach, I've seen something that makes me bang my head.

Business owners are more than willing to throw money at new, unproven tactics when instead they would be better served investing the relatively small amount of time it would take to fix the holes in their processes that are **leaking profits**…often directly into their competitors' bucket.

I'm going to disclose the six areas I've found where you can quickly seal the holes in your profit bucket, and substantially grow your profits.

Profit Growth Tactic 1: *Lead Generation* – most business owners give little to no thought about a real lead generation tactic. You may spend a lot on advertising, but that does not equate to a lead generation plan.

To have an actual tactical plan you need three things…**first**, a clear, written definition of **exactly** who your target market is (see chapter 1 of my book, **"Profit and Cash Flow Marketing…Fast"**, available at *RonHequet.com or Amazon.com*).

Second, you need a lead magnet that instantly attracts your ideal prospect.

Third, you must have a way to measure the effectiveness of any media that you're using (clicks, likes and retweets is not lead generation).

Simply getting clear on these three things will save you thousands of dollars while attracting more of your ideal prospects.

Profit Growth Tactic 2: *Lead Capture* – I recently went to a new restaurant near Fort Worth. I heard about it from a friend, and I enjoyed it. My waiter asked if I had been there before and, when I said "no", he went on to tell me about the restaurant in a well-prepared speech.

However, during my entire time in the restaurant they never tried to collect my contact information so that they could continue to stay in touch with me and offer me an incentive to return.

They, like many businesses, maybe yours too, are operating on a strategy of '**hope**' and that is a **bad** strategy. They '**hope**' that I liked it enough that I'll return. In fact, I may, but it's not the only restaurant I like and the chance of me returning to their restaurant diminishes every day that I don't have contact with them. Plus, they have no way to connect with me because they didn't even try to get my contact information.

You **must** capture customer / client / prospect contact information. You can do this online, in-person, or by phone. It's easy, yet most don't even try and depending on the size of your business it could cost you tens or even hundreds of thousands of dollars.

Profit Growth Tactic 3: *Non-Buyer Follow-Up* – This is the **greatest** area of opportunity for 97% of the businesses I have worked with. They don't have a system, an automated process to follow up with prospects to turn them into customers.

Once you have captured a prospect's contact information, you now can **create a campaign** that consistently moves customers who didn't immediately purchase your product / service to become a customer of your business. And the higher the cost of your product / service, the more important this tactic is.

You need to put a *well-planned* **on-line and off-line** follow-up campaign in place for those customers who are initially interested but not yet ready to 'buy'.

For example, this campaign could include emails, texts, phone calls, postcards and newsletters. And I believe it should include all of these. If you don't have this system in place in your business, you are probably **letting 30%-70%** of your potential customers / clients *buy from your competitors*.

Profit Growth Tactic 4: *Conversion of Customers / Clients* – This is where you can add to your profit without adding a single dollar of expense to your business! Assume each day you have 100 prospects coming to your website, contacting your office, coming into your store or however people encounter your business.

Can you tell me, out of those 100 people, what percentage will do business with you? If you can't respond to me with definite knowledge of that percent, **you need to figure that out...fast.**

Next, you must implement strategies to increase that number. Many times, it's as easy as putting simple processes in place to help that person buy from you or buy **more** from you.

Imagine you're a dentist and a patient come in for teeth cleaning. Do you have scripts in place to sell them other products or services? Do you assume they have the best toothbrush, the best toothpaste; they don't need fluoride or want whitening? How much is it costing you in lost profits to make those assumptions?

Profit Growth Tactic 5: *Repeat Business* – I read that Domino's Pizza has an app that customers can use to order pizza on-line, and it also sends notifications to those subscribed, with special offers. This allows them to turn a slow night for their stores into a busy night.

Your business should have in place a campaign to consistently keep in touch with your past customers / clients and patients. This is another example of how most businesses run on '**hope**'. Do you '**hope**' your past customers will remember you when they need another widget and have not in the meantime been attracted by a competitor?

This too should be a multi-media campaign using on-line and off-line elements to consistently **provide value** and give your customers a reason to return.

Profit Growth Tactic 6: *Referrals* – Almost no business does this well. While many come across **'referrals by chance',** almost none generate a steady stream of **'referrals by design'.**

However, when I ask most business owners the source of their best leads, they will predictably say it's those that were referred to a past customer, client or patient.

What if you, weekly, monthly or even quarterly, provided your past customers with the reasons they need to become an **'unpaid sales army'** by giving them useful reports, emails or gifts AND specific instructions **(call to action)** on exactly how to introduce others to your business? It's such an easy tactic, but have you given this tactic the slightest thought or effort?

Plugging these six holes into your leaky profit bucket will most of the time provide you with all the growth your company can handle, and many times, more than you're looking for!

Warning: *this is not simple, but it's not hard.* It just requires a commitment of time and effort on your part to develop and execute each of these six tactics.

Power In the Book

'Create a positive impact on business, write a book'

Despite the fouled up attempt to construct another headquarters in New York City, Amazon CEO Jeff Bezos has a great track record with seeing into and maybe creating the future. Many years ago, he looked into his crystal ball, consulted with trend managers, deciphered and analyzed all the data and saw the future of publishing.

His prophecy...*hold on to your hat*...was **the book!** Not an e-book, dig iBook or any other kind of book. Just a good old-fashioned book, **created with paper and ink** and there is no shortage of evidence to support that forecast.

During 2015-2019, Amazon opened 17 brick-and-mortar bookstores; from their first Seattle location, to the one that opened in Los Angeles. While the book is not immune to the forces of the digital world, Amazon's surprising move indicates that the book has been able to combat and to a point overcome those forces.

The Association of American Publishers reported that **revenue from hardback books increased 6.9%** compared to previous years, *and at the same time* **revenue from e-books declined 3.6%**. Also, the American Booksellers Association reported a 31% increase in companies and 49.6% increase in the number of physical stores over the previous 9 years.

One of the most effective and profitable tools you can have been a byline on the cover of a book.

I can testify to that; I am currently working on my 6th book. Being able to call yourself an author opens an untold number of opportunities to establish a perceived level of authority and expertise. It can help you generate more leads and grow your business.

Bloomberg did a survey of business-book authors and according to the results, **96% of the authors** that participated said they *achieved a significant positive impact on their business* from writing a book.

An essay in the Wall Street Journal, "Don't Burn Your Books – Print is Here to Stay," the writer Nicholas Carr says that 'readers of weightier fare, i.e. business books, seem to prefer the heft and long lastingness of what you and I still call **'real books'**.

I concur, I just received a copy of 'Throughput Economics, Making Good Management Decisions', co-authored by client and friend Henry F. Camp.

"Lovers of ink and paper, take heart", Carr says…
"Reports of the death of the printed book may be exaggerated."

Release the 'Power of Profitability'

What does leadership and profit have in common? A lot, really! Good to great leaders are very social. They meet, eat together and play together. They remain cohesive as a group or family and have been referred to as a wolf pack.

Although management hierarchies vary in size, the averages are 5 and the most successful care for, trust and respect each other. *Isn't being cared for, trusted and respected also important to every employee of every successful organization?*
Without caring, trust and respect, profitability suffers!

Each member of the management team has specific responsibilities, and each knows how **stepping up to their responsibilities contributes to profitability**.

The top leader, CEO, as the name / title suggests, leads this team and is ultimately responsible for the profitability of the organization by placing the needs of the business before their personal needs.

This leadership team must *release the* **'Power of Profitability'** from their team members. A leader's people's skills play a vital role in determining whether team members have a positive attitude, enjoy being at work and how they feel about the organization overall.

Don't 'talk the talk', execute and 'walk the walk.

Profit Plan

Part 4

Leadership

Act and Be a Winner

"Change in behavior cannot take place without a change in belief." – Ron Hequet

It is true that character is determined by what we are on the inside, not by our appearance on the outside. Even criminals dress well.

However, consider a particular character shortfall or the desire to enhance a particular character trait...it is a fact that if I forcibly act out in that manner, that trait will eventually change my behavior.

Today, most people are driven by feelings (emotion). They disregard facts, don't have belief in anything that causes a loss of control and make decisions on action based upon how they feel.

For example: I may not 'feel' like running errands for my aged mother (fictional), who is unappreciative, overbearing, constantly complains and always reminds me that I am not good enough. Who would 'feel' like doing anything for someone like that?

But the **'fact'** is that she is not capable of doing certain things. And for me to **'believe'** that running those errands is the right thing to do, I must **'act'** regardless of how I **'feel'**.

And what about your pompous, unfair, prejudicial boss, a co-worker who has wronged you or the neighbor whose dog leaves a daily gift on your lawn.

Even married couples don't always 'feel' in love. In fact, many marriages are hanging on by a thread because one or both have not 'acted' in a way that creates the feeling of love. And it is made worse by the 'fact' that no one wants to be the first to 'act'.

If one would recognize the **'fact'** that love is a verb, **believe'** that action is the remedy and then **'act'**, the love **feelings** will follow and who's the winner?

Like my example of the train, 'fact' is the engine and power that drives reality and truth. And if we 'believe and act' on 'fact', the desired 'feeling' will follow. *Have you ever seen a train driven by Caboose?*

What happens when you stand on ceremony, put yourself first and harden against 'facts' (truth)? You'll 'believe' you are justified based on your 'feelings', but you are not seen as a **winner**.

To alter this self-centered, losing position, I use the **"I am a winner"** action affirmations.

The list below is certainly not exhaustive, so add any that apply to you. If you **'act'** like a **'winner'**, you'll come to **'believe'** it and then you'll **'feel'** like a **'winner'**.

✓ I solved a problem.

✓ I helped someone who needed it.

✓ I donated to a charity, and no one knows.

✓ I know I made a difference today with no reward.

✓ I taught someone how to do something.

✓ I brought a smile to someone's face.

✓ I told the truth today.

✓ I completed a goal.

✓ I am healthier than most.

✓ I am a winner.

To 'Feel' like a 'Winner'; accept the 'Fact' that you are a 'Winner', then 'Believe' and 'Act' like a 'Winner'.

"Winners give more than they receive at work and at play."

2 Wealth Attraction Principles

Invest In Your Future Achievement

In order for me to achieve your strategy for any year and **will achieve**, (not 'hope to' or 'try to'), reassign your time for the upcoming year.

Yes, reassigning i.e. it was already an allocated routine and plan, but a couple of changes in your business and personal life strategy require reassignment and execution of your time schedule.

In my seminar **"Minutes Matter ©"** I share with the audience that I can tell you what I am doing at 2:30 in the afternoon, 45 days from now. Many roll their eyes, thinking 'how boring his life must be'. But that's the wrong mindset. My time is "invested". I invest my *time and money* in *work and play*.

Is it any wonder why people are where they are…having not achieved their goals when they haven't "invested" in themselves or in preparing? They complain, but they haven't "invested" in a personal coaching program…attended a seminar…signed up for a teleseminar…or (fill in the blank).

Anyone with that mindset will never attract wealth at any level. It is never an expense when you invest money toward you or your business – it is *"an investment in your future achievement"*.

Now, I know what you are thinking, "That's great Ron but this is not the right time…" I regularly encounter people for whom the excuse is…the time isn't right…I need to wait until I can afford it…when things turn around.

Read carefully – Unless you 'invest' in your own development, the time will never be right, you'll never be able to afford it, and things will never turn around. That is a poverty mind-set usually held by those who are too cheap, too lazy or think it's too good to be true. Welcome to the other 97%.

Life happens in tandem; otherwise, we wouldn't claim to be 'multitasking'. Therefore, consider an investment in yourself as a concurrent priority. It is akin to putting your own oxygen mask first, the better off you are, the more able you are to help others.

Chris Galloway, an associate with my firm, has been with me for over 20 years. Besides being good at what he does, his efforts allow me to focus on what I do best so that we are able to achieve our strategy by following the 2 wealth attraction principles that I know are essential to success, however it's defined.

Make Decisions from Where You Want to Be, Not from Where You Are!

Stay Focused on The Future Payoff, Not the Current Cost!

3% - No Matter What!

"Obstacles to your objectives should be viewed as steps to achievement."

Just before I started my first company, my father used to tell me; if you're not making mistakes, you're not doing anything.

Over the years, I took my mistakes and failures personally – as some sort of deficiency, a missing skill set, being unlucky or some other lack of talent. I had to learn and subsequently accept that failure is a necessary component of achievement.

Failure or making mistakes is just a delay, a short detour and can only be avoided, as my father used to say, by doing nothing. And that is what distinguishes 3% of the population from the 97% who give up, stay with the status quo, or do nothing.

The 3% achievers are further driven toward their strategy / goals by learning from their mistakes and failure. Joe Paterno, head coach of the Penn State football team, was asked what he thought when his team lost a game. He replied, "Losing was probably good, since that was how the players could learn what they were doing wrong."

Often, achievers are viewed as having lucky breaks or inherited their success. Almost always a lucky break is being in the right place at the right time and being prepared. For me, I must create my luck. How do I do that; by investing in myself through study, hard work and preparation, so when the opportunity presents itself, I am ready to execute, and nothing stands in the way.

3% No Matter What; in a briefcase, there is a million in cash. The briefcase is located about a 1-hour drive from where you are now. If you make it, I will hand you the briefcase, and it's all yours. All you must do is get there within the next 90 minutes. There is, however, one caveat. Just one second late and the deal is off, no excuses! So, when are you going to go for it?

Most would jump into the car and start driving to the briefcase. During the trip, all excited, you're thinking about how you're going to spend the money. Then traffic comes to a halt. There has been a major 5 car accident between you and the briefcase, and there is no way off the freeway or around the accident.

Now what? Would you give up? Or would you get out of your car and run, hire a helicopter; do anything, no matter what, to find some other way of getting to the briefcase on time?

In contrast, let's imagine that you are driving to an appointment with your hair stylist (men – assuming you have hair). The traffic again halts because of the same accident. What would you do in that case?

Most would probably give up, call and reschedule. What's the difference between these two scenarios? The difference is known by the 3% of achievers.

If the *what* (strategy) is important enough, the *how* (tactics) is usually not a problem and may only be a delay or detour to learning, hard work, preparation and then execution.

Now apply this to your career, your business.

- ✓ Do you have a strategy?

- ✓ Have you prepared?

- ✓ Do you have a tactical plan of execution?

- ✓ Are you afraid of making mistakes and possible failure?

3% of us have a strategy, are prepared, have a plan and are not afraid, but determined to achieve, **no matter what!**

Do It...Now

Part I

"Change in behavior cannot take place without a change in belief."

No, it's not a version of the Nike tag. It was first said by W. Clement Stone. Along with the likes of Napoleon Hill, they discovered that **one of the secrets of achievers** was that procrastination or the delay of deciding was not part of their character.

I am not suggesting that decisions weren't often proceeded by due diligence, but they didn't get bogged down in 'paralysis of analyses or the negative vibes from naysayers. When the President asked a top scientist if it were possible to put a man on the moon, his response was *'all we need is to decide to do it and then act'*.

'DO IT NOW'...is an affirming, self-actuating statement that puts you into action. Today, begin to develop this habit by applying it in the little things.

Let's imagine you have a phone call to make, and you've delayed because that's your way, and you have put off making the call.

When 'DO IT NOW' comes from your subconscious, **ACT**, make the call, DO IT NOW!

Do It...Now

Part 2

"Make a purposeful decision to control your mind and actions to achieve the positive." ©

William James, the well-known psychologist said, *"Sow an action and reap a habit; sow a habit and reap a character; sow a character and reap a destiny."*

Each of these points is a 'choice'. Yes, the approach of 'DO IT NOW' is **a conscious choice**. Not doing it now is a choice as well. You are forced to make a choice, whether you admit it or not.

I don't know many who could be classified as 'early risers', but think of what could be accomplished by getting out of bed just 15 minutes before your normal time, i.e. time alone, time with your spouse, your kids, to pray, to read or listen to achievement books / CD's / DVD's, THUMB DRIVES etc. This was made easier for me by going to bed earlier.

An Army General I once knew, already an early riser, wanted to get up an hour earlier. So, he set his alarm 1 minute earlier every day for 60 days.

This allowed his body and mind to adjust to the earlier hour over a period. However, if you set the alarm earlier and then reach over and turn it off, that's **not the right mind set** for 'DO IT NOW!'

People who never achieve the 'mind-set' of 'DO IT NOW', are late for work, buy a birthday or anniversary gift at the last minute and function from the never-ending 'to-do' list, scratching out one line and adding three.

That's 'do it tomorrow' which ends up being 'do it not'.

Many years ago, in one of my businesses, my leadership was demonstrated by being an exemplary in sales; not to mention the need, the business was going through a rough period.

We kept a card file on prospective customers and followed up with them until enough time went by that we considered them no longer a viable prospect.

I selected 20 prospect cards from the 'dead' file and diligently prepared a special presentation, just for them. Although the 'DO IT NOW' concept was not part of my make-up at the time, I had applied its positive principles without knowing.

Why, because **it had to happen now**. My positive approach won the day. Within six weeks, I had closed 12 substantial sales.

'DO IT NOW'...is an affirming, self-actuating statement that puts you into action.

Achieve Growth with Achievers

Part I

"Achievers know how to swim against the current." ©

With the right, selective, hiring strategy, even the smallest of businesses have achieved appreciable growth; both top line and bottom line. You *can* hire a single salesperson or a team that *will* launch business growth. Most businesses use the wrong measures for selecting salespeople. I admit, I am not the only person in the business arena who knows how, but do you?

✓ How to draw achievers to your organization and shun the lightweights in less than 5 minutes.

✓ How to uncover their flaws *prior* to hiring. Most only discover a person's problems after they have been hired and underachieved.

✓ How to know the distinctive character traits of over-achievers and why you should hire for their character profile and not the resume.

An overachiever is a person who can be in bad organization, with inadequate support, almost no training, and within a few months, they end up outselling your previous best. There are two main traits that push an achiever, and they are both imperative when you find them and that is the **ability to bond** with anyone and have a **strong sense of self**.

Achievers have a need to bond with others (and not just prospects), to find something agreeable about everyone they meet. This achiever, like the energizer bunny, just keeps going and going, trying to find ways to serve and to please the customer.

The interview experience must be specifically designed to discover their ability to bond.

Having a strong sense of self, and I don't mean the emotionally driven 'kumbaya' self- esteem, but the self-confidence possessed by over-achievers. Only a person with a strong sense of self-worth goes back to a customer eight times after the customer has said no.

Folks, who lack a strong sense of self, go down the road after the first rejection, because they fear rejection and depend on price or other related bait to close a sale.

I have read that **52% of salespeople stop after one rejection**, and only 4% will try 4 or more times. But the current gurus will tell you that **it takes 8+ turndowns just to get a meeting**. And the difference between a person who will get a 'no' one time and quit or get that same 'no' 10 times and never quit, is simply a strong sense of self.

It's possible to train certain people to face rejection again and again (I've done that), or you can hire the achiever who (without that training), is just made that way.

Another quality of an achiever is **self-actuation**. Isn't it great when you hire someone who takes it upon themselves to do a workaround or expand and enhances every task you give them? This self-motivation and need to bond can make these people seem to come on too strong. But do not let that boldness turn you off. That is the model made up of a sale over-achiever.

Achieve Growth with Achievers

Part 2

"You don't get to the top and then become an achiever; it's the other way around." ©

With the right, selective, hiring strategy even the smallest of businesses have achieved appreciable growth; both top line and bottom line. Most businesses use the wrong measures for selecting salespeople.

I'm offering specifics in what to write in a job posting, how to handle the phone interview, who gets face time and the best tactics for the in-person interview, to truly discover the achiever for your organization.

1. One of the first ground rules is that age and what a person has accomplished are not germane. I've hired early twenty-year-olds who have out-sold sales veterans. One of my best finds came from a shopping mall. As I entered the mall, he was replacing a sign in the large directory fixture. I was looking for a watch repair store, but I didn't know the name of the store, so I asked him for help.

    He blew me away with enthusiasm. He not only told me the name of the business but took me to it, all the while having a conversation along the way; asking if I was from the area and so on, e.g. **he bonded with me**.

    Another great find was a 60+year-old who never had a bad day and had a way of making the customer experience memorable. So, don't be concerned about age or background.

2. Next, you must design your ad posting to attract these scarce individuals. The ad or posting is like this:

SUPERSTARS ONLY: Do not call unless you are an overachiever and can prove it. Call 12-2 only!

No request for a resume. Don't run the ad or post the opening unless you are prepared to spend two hours a day for five straight days call screening. Do not give this task to HR or delegate it to your assistant. Do not 'Hire Too Fast, or Fire Too Slow' and remember that **10's hire 9's, 9's hire 8's, 8's hire 7's**, etc.

3. When you take the call, apologize for being short and to the point, but explain that you are overrun with responses to the ad and then say, *"Tell me why you think you're a superstar."*

After their response then deliberately act unimpressed and a bit gruff. If they're intimidated over the phone, cross their name off the list. **An achiever will not be intimidated**.

If they can't talk their way into getting an interview, why would you believe they'll ever talk their way into a customer / client? Save yourself a lot of time, cross off the weak persona from the beginning.

If you interview candidates as the nice person, you are, you won't be able to challenge their resolve. You'll hire this nice person and find out down the road that they can't close a sale, and shy away from the big sales opportunities because of a weak self-esteem. With this approach you find out right away how they handle rejection. This will save you time and money.

4. At the face-to-face interview, begin by giving them every opportunity to show their best side, helping them relax. You will be friendly and a great listener. The goal of this part of the conversation is to get to know the real person.

At the start of the interview, you must tell the candidate that they don't have to answer any questions they don't want to. Tell them that you hire based upon a 'psychological profile' rather than their resume. That gives you the opportunity to really probe into how they became who they really are.

Additionally, this part of the interview tests that **'ability to bond'** a characteristic I wrote about in part 1. If they remain or become 'formal' during this part, you don't have a natural bonder.

Ask about their childhood, their mother, their father, and questions about how they grew up. Ask for situations where they stepped up or overachieved in some way. If they become uncomfortable, this is not a superstar. **Superstars like to bond with others**.

Next, you may think you've found an achiever, but you'll often be surprised when you **'confront'**. Say, *"You seem like a nice person, but I don't get the impression you're really a superstar."* Be polite but imply that they don't seem to have what it takes. Most people will **cave**. Suddenly they agree and thank you for your time.

Cut them loose. Superstars don't cave. Achievers have confidence in themselves, and nothing can convince them they can't do the job.

. The last part of hiring top talent is to offer performance-based employment, e.g. with little or no guaranteed salary. There are variables and you must be legally compliant.

Example: A client of mine offered $12.00 an hour, plus commission, and they put that in the job posting. However, the company's best salesperson earned about $94,000 annually. I asked, *"Do you want to attract achievers like your best or do you want to attract the $12.00 an hour kind of talent?"* So, they posted 'Earn as high as $100K, if you are a Superstar' in the ad. This significantly changed the type of person they began to attract.

What not to do; hire by 'committee'. Another client had the candidate interview with everyone in the department and all had to agree on the candidate, or they're not hired.

Results: When a real achiever came on the scene, nobody wanted that candidate to get the job, because they saw this person as the 'competition'.

Remember...10's hire 9's, 9's hire 8's, 8's hire 7's, etc. This company hired nice folks who couldn't sell.

The 5 Delegation Basics

"The rewards, including earning power, are great for those who lead others to success." ©

There are 5 basic steps to proper delegation of tasks and duties to existing personnel and the imperative supervision that will assure that expectations are met and success is achieved.

1. First, be very specific about the **result** that you want from the activity. The clearer you are in your own mind regarding the desired outcome (you may want to write it out), the easier it will be for you to select the right person for the job.

2. Next, select a person based on their demonstrated skill set. If the results are important to your business, this is probably **not the time to give someone a chance**. It's vital that you delegate to someone who you confidently know can deliver the desired outcome.

3. Third, **relay** to the person exactly **what** you want done, **how** you want it done (if required, and usually is) **when** it's due and the **results that you expect**. Taking the time to teach and clarify the best way to perform the task is required to ensure that the activity will be performed as you wish and on time.

4. This is **where most management falls short**. You must appoint a time(s) for reporting progress. The more important the work...I recommend that you set a deadline for completion that is a day or a week before the actual deadline. This allows for some flexibility and to adjust if necessary. Leave nothing to chance.

5. Inspect, delegation is not abdication. At the end of the day, **you're still responsible**.

If you are one of those that believes…'it's easier for me to do it myself than to teach someone else to do it'…or the all-time hit song, 'if you want it done right, do it yourself'…then **you are in the way of growing your business**.

Make a list of tasks and duties answering these questions. What task can you delegate to a subordinate? Which one of your employees can handle the assignment? **DIN** (Do it now!)

Approach to Hiring

"Achievement is an accurate reflection of approach and desire." ©

Today, with so many economic unknowns, there is nothing more important than hiring the right talent. And, if you're going to delegate that to an administrative or HR functionaries...remember, those people are, whether they would own up to it or not, bias and have an unwritten agenda that does not align with the business owner. Not to mention a lack of qualifications and 'real world' job performance experience.

Have you ever heard of anyone successful in a career and then choosing to go into HR? **Business owner, it is your job and responsibility to hire and train your employees.**

If your company cannot function day-to-day without you performing certain work, then **you own a job not a company**. I am not saying that the basic screening of job requirements, i.e. licensing, certifications, testing, etc. cannot be relegated to others, but never phone interviews or face time with an applicant. Why?

If you get the best possible mix of people working for your company, your odds of success exponentially increase. However, the best person for the job doesn't always walk right through your door.

Number 1, when searching for any key employee, you're looking for a personality that fits with your company culture.

Content and most skills can be taught and learned, but **you cannot train people to have the right approach.**

If you can find people whose approach is where, *'it's not all about them'*, and they are fun, friendly, caring and love helping others, you are on to someone qualified to be in the **'VIP 3% Winner's Circle'**.

Personality and approach are key ingredients. It is not something that always comes out in an interview…people can be shy. But you must trust your instincts, which is another reason why this process cannot be delegated. If you meet a slightly introverted person with a great personality, use your experience to pull it out of them. If you can't, turn them loose.

If you have ever attended one of my talks or seminars, you would never expect me to be a little shy off stage, but I am. It's easier with an extrovert but be wary of people being too outgoing in the pressure of interviews, wanting to impress too much.

In less than 90 days a newbie can usually know the ins and outs of their role, so if you are comfortable with their personality, then and only then look at proven skill sets. **Hire people with transferable skills**.

You'll need team players who can pitch in and try their hand at all kinds of different tasks. While specialists are sometimes necessary, adaptability should not be underrated.

Too many managers get hung up on credentials and diplomas. I only consider them after everything else and only if required.

An impressive resume doesn't necessarily mean they are the right person for the position.

Degrees count for nothing if they aren't combined with broad-ranging experience and a winning personality.
Don't be afraid of hiring a nonconformist. Somebody who thinks a little differently can see problems as opportunities and inspire creative energy within a group. Some of the best people I've hired didn't seem to fit at first but proved to be valuable in no time.

If you hire the wrong person in a key position, they can wipe out any success you've had there in no time. Promoting from within is generally a good idea, as this person will be inspired by the new role, already knows your business model, and has the trust and respect of others. At the same time beware of the *'peter principle'*, promoting a person lacking the ability to deliver. Likewise, bringing in new talent can bolster a company or department.

When organizations go through growth spurts, they often hire

several people at once and company culture and performance can suffer. Too many times you are in a desperate rush to fill an empty chair to fill a void or to take the load off others. It is worth being patient to find the right person(s), rather than making hasty decisions and taking steps backward.

Someone once said, 'it's better to have a hole *in* your team than an _ _ _ hole *on* your team'.

May I Speak with The Manager?

Lessons in Customer Experience

*A*lthough giving gifts is not the reason I celebrate Christmas, it is nonetheless part of the holiday and I truly enjoy the giving part, but not the shopping and buying part; and not because I am male.

You would think that all employees (particularly retail) would be excited to see a customer anytime, but especially since for most companies, profitability is determined by the success of the last calendar quarter, you would think they would be exceptionally eager to provide memorable service during this time.

Many years ago, my son had moved to a new home, and it didn't have a microwave oven. I went to Best Buy to buy one. Although the store was well staffed, I was ignored as I stood in the microwave oven aisle. So, I went to the help desk and told a young lady that I wanted to buy a microwave, but I had some questions. **"No problem"** she said **[a phrase that should be forbidden]**, "I will send someone right over."

A few minutes later, I'm still standing alone. I guess it's the 'business owner mentality' in me, but I get irritated with poor service and lack of follow-through. I walked back to the young lady sitting at the help desk and saw 3 blue-shirted Best Buy salespeople standing next to her desk talking and one was even texting.

Solution: Are you watching? In my retail companies, I used to walk around watching my employees (I did the same in my manufacturing, distributing or other companies). **A business owner doesn't know what's going on without being there and watching.**

Don't expect your people to innately know to do this – train your staff to be on the look-out for customers needing help. And, if you are overwhelmed with customers, communicate to those waiting (and not with the worn-out 'we'll be right with you').

Americans have developed, in the words of writer Harlan Ellison, a 'slacker mentality.' Not everyone, but in my observations, a significant number of employees, just don't seem to give a darn about their career, the company they work for, or its customers – it's just a job.

The episode at Best Buy reminded me of a business axiom I learned years ago; when someone is trying to give you money, don't make it difficult for them to do so.

Here's another 'approach' adjustment you may want to make: Have you ever been upset or disappointed in how your transaction was handled or not handled, and then asked to speak with the manager / owner? You would think that you have just asked to see their financial statements or asked to speak with the King of Siam. I have never seen or heard about that request being met with a smile and a response of 'Certainly sir, I will have him / her come to your attention right away'.

No, first it's passed to another clerk and / or a supervisor who wants to know **'what's the problem'**. This person, who may give you the results you wanted, but does so with an attitude that makes just being there totally uncomfortable, as if *you* are the customer, is the problem.

Solution: I trained all my employees and managers that if any customer ever asked to speak with the manager or the owner, that they were to get the manager directly, or give them my office phone number (I couldn't possibly be in all locations). And if that call came to the office, my assistant was trained to **never screen the call** past the fact that they were a customer.

The good news is that because of the on-going and repetitive customer experience training I conducted, a problem like that was a rare as the steaks in the meat cooler.

Business is more competitive than ever. The current recession has made both B2C and B2B customers more discerning with their money. Customers have more choices for the services and products they want to buy than at any time in recorded history. Yet when prospective buyers walk in the door or pick up the phone, so many business owners send them running, blowing the sale on the spot.

Billionaire insurance entrepreneur A.L. Williams once said: "You beat 90% of the competition just by showing up. The other 10% you must defeat in a vicious dogfight."

With the employee's counter-productive, anti-customer approach, **so many businesspeople I encounter today are losing** right out of the shoot (as in rodeo).

In doubt, you may want to ask me about assessing what you think is 'good customer service' and replacing it with a 'memorable customer experience'.

6 Ways to Recognize a supervisor

"Leadership Is Self-Leadership Applied to Others"

A person's level of adaptability is a major component to whether they will achieve in the role of supervision.

An individual who takes in information quickly is always a key plus. It's a basic requirement for taking the step into management, regardless of the industry.

However, there is a wider range of criteria among people who have grown their management career within an organization after any initial temporary period. I have observed that those employees demonstrated many of the following characteristics that today's businesses need.

Be on the lookout for...

1. *A positive, can-do approach...*
2. *Capacity to stay productive...*
3. *Ability to adapt to change...*
4. *The desire for self-improvement...*
5. *Undertaking time to assist in special projects...*
6. *Networks with strategic people.*

Fitting the Salesperson to the Customer

"If you know the combination to the achievement lock, it has to open."

Ever wore a pair of shoes that didn't fit? Placing a salesperson in the wrong selling circumstance is like an ill-fitting pair of shoes and an easy mistake to make for any business owner.

The good news is that fitting a salesperson with your company is not difficult to learn how to do and will mean the difference between achievement and failure in making a sale. Here are the basic guidelines I learned to follow in my businesses.

Profile Your Sales Staff: People who fit a sales position fall into three fundamental categories, based upon their character make-up, personality type, approach and desire.

1) **The Knowledgeable** – A 'knowledgeable', refers to their own experience helping the buyer be comfortable with him / her *and* the product / service.

The 'knowledgeable' **takes advantage of their experience and not by being warm and cuddly**. This salesperson does best when they are presenting to a cautious customer who has concerns about certain aspects of their purchasing decision.

To achieve, the 'knowledgeable' requires beneficial information; proof of the product's / service's best features and timely, truthful responses to the customer's questions or objections.

) **The Buddy** – The 'buddy' is very good at establishing relationships, very friendly, smiles and is pleasant to be around. Customers buy from this person just because they like him / her.

The chief characteristic of the 'buddy' is **their ability to establish a relationship with the buyer**. The 'buddy' succeeds most when the customer wants more from the salesperson than business, and when he / she can use amusement as a sales tool. Give the 'buddy' clear, detailed, but simple information that explains your product / service.

Pair the 'buddy' up with the 'knowledgeable', for they can have a very positive effect on one another and positive results with a customer. And, if it's applicable to your business, give the 'buddy' permission to spend money on entertainment for the buyer.

The Tiger – The 'tiger' is serious, rolling through a prospective customer list until they achieve a sale. It's a numbers game to the 'tiger', and they are typically weak when it comes to customer service and can often not capture repeat business. The 'tiger's' persistence generates sales, but sometimes creates enemies.

Tigers achieve success when they're left free to operate. **They value the freedom to close sales on the spot**. Tigers thrive on independence, latitude in margins, customer service and a simple closing process.

Execute the Fit: For all your selling environments, match the buyer with the appropriate salesperson. Be instinctive; you'll have to draw from your own assumptions about some of your buyers' wants and needs. Evaluate your sales staff. And then, identify the profile of each salesperson to fit the needs for each customer.

Fitting the right salesperson for the right situation benefits you, your business and the salesperson. Everybody wins; both the salesperson and the customer, in an environment where there is a right fit, **like a good pair of shoes**.

3 Guidelines for Value Decisions

'Improve Your Management Skills'

No one, including me, was automatically a good leader or manager, just because I owned the business. Like honing any skill set, it takes study and practice and more study and practice.

Leadership is another **'hot topic'** and this section of this issue deals with 3 guidelines that I have successfully applied to mine and others, leadership skills.

When you apply these guidelines, the right questions to ask, combined with frequent use, common sense and experience, you lay the foundation for making value decisions. However you apply these guidelines, they will help you critique decisions you are about to make, leading to a way to improve the value of your decision.

1) **Control: Are things going right?** Ask what else needs to be done to ensure efficient control and coordination to lead to the outcome I seek and so I'll know when or if I must modify my implementation or plan, because I'm not getting the results I want?

Leaders / Managers may have a different definition of control, depending upon the circumstances. And it's not uncommon for a manager to be overly concerned about consensus instead of being as concerned about whether communication is properly understood.

2) **Competence: Does everyone know what to do and how to do it?** Ask what else needs to be done so that all those involved have the required knowledge and skills to ensure effective progress?

Leaders / Managers will need to determine whether they've got the right people on the bus. And it is important to find out if coaching is needed, i.e. OJT or one on one.

3) **Condition:** Ask what must be done, if anything, to ensure that team leaders, who must execute will have a positive, getter done, approach?

Leaders / Managers should see to it that policies and procedures are in writing and in place to reduce stress over having to interpret how decisions are to be carried out. And are there tangible rewards for a job well done.

A *'thank you'* for a job well done can go a long way in boosting effective results. Give some thought to this very simple gesture and you would be surprised at how many things you do for which they can be thanked, which improves your leadership / management skills **and brings value to your decisions that others execute**.

How to Build Your Brand Internally

'Employees Can Be the Key'

When establishing and growing your brand, employees are an important resource, since they are the ones who engage with your customers every day. Here are **5 keys to installing your brand with your staff**.

A. Assess Employee Knowledge: Conduct staff meetings to explain your branding vision with your entire team. Provide employees with the opportunity to offer feedback, so any concerns can be met head-on.

B. Align Staff with Your Brand: Develop a team of brand supporters from the beginning. Recruit talent whose skill set lends itself to reinforcement of your brand. Make brand identity a key in all team member training programs.

C. Energize Your Team: Tell employees that you are committed to delivering on your brand and they have the authority to do so within their organizational roles. Encourage creativity on how to manifest the brand within their functions. They will be drawn in and proud of what the brand really means.

D. Recognition and Praise: Give incentives for those that take that extra step to reinforce your brand with customers, by offering prizes and for sure, recognition at company meetings and events.

E. Quantify Results: Reach out to your front-line staff to have relay conversations they have with customers. And check-in with customers and prospective customers to verify that your brand values are being communicated.

If your employees respect your organization and your brand, that message will come through to your customers.

Leadership Resolve and Its Achilles Heel

'Lead From the Inside Out'

You can't plan to have resolve, but you can **choose to be resolute**. Resolving is a quality that makes your other qualities possible. There's no money back guarantee for leaders.

You can resolve to do your best, and still not achieve your goal. There can be unconsidered contingencies that are outside your control. It is also true that all **leadership qualities taken to excess can become a vice**, and your strengths can become a weakness.

You must **resolve to restrain your own sense of self-importance**. It's imperative that you have the modesty and grace to declare that you (and I) depend on others, as well as how they depend upon you.

Every day is another opportunity to resolve to lead in this way. The chance might come in a conversation with a team member, or in a group meeting.

But, when you resolve to lead inclusive of others, you choose long term significance over short term success.

Are any of the below your Achilles Heel?

- ✓ Believe you know it all...

- ✓ Believe you're in charge...

- ✓ Believe the rules don't apply to you...

- ✓ Believe you'll never fail...

- ✓ Believe you did it by yourself...

- ✓ Believe you are better than the 'little people'...

- ✓ Believe you are the organization...

Do You Hire Attributes or Skills?

'How to Get Rewards to the Top and Bottom Line'

In the past, Southwest Airlines received a job application every two seconds. Given the real talent shortage these days, you'd think they'd grab many of those applicants, particularly the ones with resumes in engineering and technology. But, even before their first flight in June of '71, they've been very selective in their hiring process.

Years ago, they evaluated 287,422+ resumes, chose 102,112 of those to interview, and **hired** only 6,582, or **less than 2% of all applicants**.

Of course, an employer must work to keep good employees engaged by offering opportunities for development in a strategy-driven culture. But from the start you must select people whose values are in line with your organization.

I read that Southwest Airlines **doesn't hire based on skills** but on 3 attributes: **a warrior spirit** (a desire to excel, act and persevere); **a servant's heart** (putting others first, proactively serve customers); and **a have-fun attitude** (passion, joy and not taking themselves too seriously).

These attributes are clearly defined and described in every one of their job (position) descriptions. *[I have never liked the term **'job'** description. There is a difference between and job and a position.]*

Have you named and defined what attributes are a prerequisite to be employed by your organization? Have you designed your selection and interviewing approach around those attributes? Your approach shouldn't be… **'I'll know it when I see it.'** It should be more along the lines of…**'does this person already live our culture?'**

Naturally, certain positions require specific skills. Southwest is not going to hire a pilot who aligns with all their key attributes but can't fly a plane! However, if it comes down to two equally qualified candidates the one with your key attributes should receive the job offer.

But **here is where most employers blunder;** when a position has gone unfilled too long, they hire a qualified (skill set) candidate who doesn't possess the right values and attributes.

Your development and promotion systems must also be based on your company values. In annual performance reviews, your employees should be rated not just on results but on how they get results.

Using the Southwest example, employees are rated for their warrior spirit, servant's heart and fun-loving attitude. And people being considered for leadership roles should be an exemplar of those attributes.

Yes, it takes time and effort to hire correctly, but **the rewards to both the top and bottom line are huge**.

And unless you are a large organization, the owner(s) and the very top people should conduct this process; not relegated to HR.

If you get this right, you'll be attracting the best talent *(they will seek you out)*, and you will retain your best people.

An employee survey at Southwest, when asked whether the employee felt like their job was *'just a job'* 'a steppingstone', or 'a calling', nearly 75% selected, *'a calling'*, and 86% said they were proud to work for Southwest.

Hiring for the right values and attributes will be **considered success from your employee's viewpoint as well as yours!**

Why New Businesses Fail

'Examine Your Market'

We all know the success stories of Facebook, Airbnb, Twitter, Uber and others, including small businesses you could recall. But **only 5% of new businesses do it**.

In a detailed review of over 2000 new businesses financed with venture capital it reveals that more than 95% of the startups fail to see a return on investment. Some 40% of US startups liquidate all assets, with investors losing all their money.

Why? Because the **old management methods** of a good plan, a solid strategy and thorough market research **don't work**, because they operate with too much uncertainty. An analysis shows you the top 20 reasons why startups fail.

Insufficient market need	42%	Ran out of cash	29%
Poor management team	23%	Beaten by competitors	19%
Price/cost issues	18%	Poor product	17%
Poor/no Business model	17%	Poor marketing	14%
Ignore customers	14%	Product mistimed	13%
Lose focus	13%	Disharmony w/investors	13%
Bad pivot	10%	Passion fades	9%
Poor location	9%	No investor interest	8%
Legal issues	8%	Did not use advisors	8%
Burn out	8%	**Failure to pivot**	7%

I have observed and the analysis shows that **there is seldom only one reason why start-ups or undeveloped businesses fail**, this is why the list exceeds 100%.

The main reason why these businesses fail is that the founders have a 'big idea' and come up with a so-called solution for something where there is no market need or demand.

A successful business needs four ingredients: relevant market need, a marketing dominating position, a viable business plan and an advisor on board who has successfully founded a business.

Examine your company today and ensure that none of these issues are creeping in and your market demand does not decline.

Be Selective in Seeking Advice

'Can You Teach Me to Ride A Bike?'

During a client coaching call, my client told me that a sales rep advised them to drop a particular line of products, claiming that his brand would make up the difference and increase profitability. I couldn't believe my client even considered the advice.

Why do we listen to people who have no sound reason, no experiential validation for giving you advice? I've heard that someone's idea for an electric fork was solidly supported by a random seatmate on the flight from Dallas to Chicago, or someone who has given up their idea of expanding their business because a member in an association meeting thought it was impossible.

Remember *Serena Williams*? She had a tennis coach just for her serve. He does not play at her caliber of championship competition, but he does know a lot about serves **and can produce a real mean serve**.

If a person in my VIP 3% Winner's Circle™ critiques my business, I'm listening, but if a person who has never founded a company and has no proven history offers advice, I'm not.

You must be very careful about whom you choose to listen to. Sometimes you're listening to long ago comments from family or friends which have no past or current basis but are nonetheless **preventing you from moving forward**.

You may be listening to static noise or anxious communication which you are misinterpreting as supportive. Critics have their role in theater, literature, art, and so on. They are usually trained and informed about the content of their specialty.

But **I've always maintained it's easier to criticize than create**. They are merely voicing opinion and personal bias, often sadly misinformed and lack experience. And some practice projection, the psychological condition that if they couldn't achieve goals like yours, well, neither can you, because you're certainly not more talented than they are!

Make sure the people from whom you accept advice and feedback have demonstrated excellence in the realm of your goals and objectives. I've never known anyone who can teach someone to ride a bike without having ridden one themselves.

How to Defeat Time Management Paralysis

'A Powerful 5-Step Approach'

Is this you; emails, voicemails, and your to-do list keeps growing. **'Time Management Paralysis'** is a common issue for entrepreneurs, especially those who like the stimulation of new ideas and different insights.

The only way to deal with this paralysis is to focus on one thing at a time, and make sure your big projects are specifically clear-cut.

Here's an example. My personal big initiative right now is to create my new books. I'm committed to doing whatever necessary to write the project. Everything else is a potential distraction from that objective.

Even so, I can't just shut down the rest of my business activity to solely work on the writing. Instead, I have to proficiently manage the inflow of tasks every day...all without losing sight of my main objective.

To manage this problem, I've developed a **powerful 5-step approach**: *Discard, Delegate, Outsource, Schedule, and Act Now*.

Here's how you make it work:

1. Discard: As soon as a new idea, email, text, or insight gets put in front of you, ask yourself, is this truly imperative?' If the answer is 'no', then discard it immediately. Taking this simple first step, you will eliminate loads of distractions from your business activity objectives, before they start to change your focus.

2. **Delegate:** If you can't discard something that comes your way, your next move is to delegate. Whether it's having a member of your team research a new idea you'd like to know more about, or letting your assistant respond to emails, return phone calls and schedule meetings for you; delegating can save you time, energy, and focus for the big project.

3. **Outsource:** If you don't have someone who you can delegate tasks to, it's time to outsource. Whether it is a virtual assistant or a vendor, get creative about how to utilize outside resources, so that you can maintain your own priorities.

4. **Schedule:** Although it is less often than you think, sometimes there are activities that only you can perform. When this happens, *smart scheduling* is your most powerful tool. Don't allow yourself to take on new tasks that only you can perform right then; instead, schedule them for a specific time in the future. The key is to make sure the future activity doesn't interfere with your current priorities.

5. **Act now:** If all else fails and an activity demands your immediate attention, then act right now to deal with it.

6. Don't procrastinate; just get it done now, so that you can move forward on your truly important work.

At the end of the day, it's important not to let the daily inflow of emails, texts, voice mail and other distractions control your activity.

For instance, I only do email twice a day; first thing in the morning and the last thing at night. If it were truly important, I would have gotten a phone call to my office.

Never check your messages constantly or change what you are doing when you receive a message. Remember to focus on your own objectives, not the agendas of others. Commit to moving forward with a specific action each day, week, and month...and stick to it.

This Discard & Delegate 5-Step approach will make you more productive and efficient. If you're ready to defeat your **'Time Management Paralysis',** it's time to implement this simple approach...**NOW!**

The Big Obstacle to Growing Your Business

'Don't Post...Recruit'

The survey by Chief Executive Magazine of CEO's discloses that there are multi-thousands of unfilled employment positions.

'Posting job openings is a second-rate strategy. You need no other proof than the fact that it is the norm that everybody has defaulted to. Remember, the majority is almost always wrong.

Admittedly, my clients had the same problem.

Case Study: My consulting work with my client in Waterford, Michigan...in less than 36 months we have made his company very profitable, almost eliminated debt and has good cash flow.

Naturally, yes, that's what I do. [Please excuse my shameless self-indorsement from *"America's Leading Profit and Cash Flow Marketing Strategist"*], (inject your smile and laughter here and rolling of eyes). I wanted to expand his company but found it extremely difficult because of a lack of available talent.

So, we turned to referral and recruit from his top team members and even other friends / business owners (not in his industry niche) to recommend *'Winners'* they consider worthy.

The key word: **RECRUIT!**

Not job postings, not even advertising the openings. I learned that less than 3% of jobs that are posted on internet sites are awarded through that system. 97% are obtained through **who you know, not what you know**.

Due to this serious and growing shortage of qualified candidates, you will have to hire a lot more based on enthusiasm, attitude, character, coachability, etc., rather than aptitude or experience.

Remember what I have always said, '**You can always teach content; you cannot teach enthusiasm.'**

Hence, you need a direct-response based recruiting system – a funnel – a screening process – and a great on-boarding system.

While I admit that this is a real problem, i.e. growth is obstructed by the lack of qualified talent.

The NFIB (National Federation of Independent Businesses) annual business owner outlook survey scored 107.6, the 2nd highest in its 51+ year history. NFIB president said, "Main Street is on fire (in a good way) again."

NFIB also reports finding qualified employees is the top problem facing small business owners. **"Out-bidding other employers, competing for the same employee candidates, is not the answer."**

You must think 'outside the box (I hate that phrase), think creatively, to open opportunities for search, recruiting from ranks not looking for a job, for sure finding talent and recruiting them, getting your best people to refer and recruit, getting your customers to refer candidates, and then being prepared to 'invest' in training on job performance specifics (content).

I strongly recommend you offer a cash reward ($500.00 or whatever is appropriate) **for a successful referral / hire.**

You will have to **'MARKET'** your job opportunities *with a multifaceted description of reasons to choose your company*. Also, supply and demand influence your profitability.

When the job market has millions more open job positions than there are creditable candidates to fill them, your business plan must include a labor plan, i.e. where wages are a variable percentage to sales. If not, your profitability and cash flow will deteriorate.

The High Cost of Distractions

'Limit Your Non-Productive Behaviors'

In one of my recent **VIP 3% Winners Circle™ Mastermind session**, I asked members to write on a white-board the *'bad habits'* they wanted to overcome. One wrote 'Squirrel', another wrote 'Bright Shiny Objects', 'Too Many Priorities', and another 'I Say Yes to Too Many Things'.

'Scattered Focus' was the topic of the day.

Your ability to singularly focus on your core business will fundamentally determine how successful it will be. 10 years ago, out of necessity, my firm established a strategy and tactical plan to grow 5X over a two-year period.

Our success was attributed to an undistracted focus on the goal for two years. Yes, I made some minor modifications occasionally, but overall, we kept *the main thing the main thing*. Some entrepreneurs can't keep the main thing the main thing for 2 minutes.

Why is that? You, an entrepreneur, are creative and **comfortable in saying 'yes' rather than saying 'no'**. You may also think that the more products you offer, *the more services you provide, the more money you will make*. **WRONG!**

When Steve Jobs returned to Apple in 1997, he fueled Apple's great revival by reducing the product line of 20+ products to 4.

It is much more important to have a **'stop doing' list as opposed to a 'to-do list'**.

So, what can you do? Examine your business under a microscope, *(or engage me to do it)*. Analyze the products and services you offer. Remember the Pareto Principle, which states that approximately 80% of results are from 20% of effects.

For instance, 80% of your revenue is 20% of your products. 80% of your sales come from 20% of your sales staff.

This principle is everywhere.

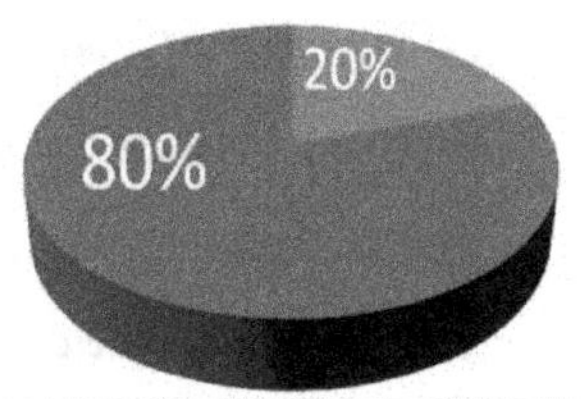

Which 20% of your products and / or services are netting you 80% of your results? After this look under the microscope, cut the 80% that only produces 20%.

This examination will cause you to create a much leaner business. Next, invest the time, energy and resources that you liberated and focus on integrating them into the 20% that provides you the 80% return.

In the **VIP 3% Winners Circle™** I work to create accountability amongst the members so we can challenge each other from distractions which lead to non-productive behaviors.

The # 1 Obstacle to Growth

'Competing to Get Employees Worth Having'

The gloomy side of our current economy is that it is reported that there are 7 million more jobs than there are unemployed or under-employed folks to fill those jobs. This affects small businesses most. The problem is particularly grave at the low-level jobs, at the counter, at the front desk and on the phones.

This problem **dictates unconventional hiring and recruiting efforts**, not just advertising open jobs. For example, Taco Bell is conducting 'hiring parties' at their restaurants, including free food, drinks, and actual humans – store managers and corporate executives on-site to meet, mingle and speak with job seekers...*instead of the usual request for applications and resumes submitted online.*

This past April and May, these parties were held at 600 different restaurants. The company promotes its **'Start with Us – Stay with Us'** plan. This is corroborated by the fact that 80% of its leadership level positions at restaurants and all the way into corporate are filled by promotions from within.

If your business is one of the many, and probably is, who need people to grow, you are going to have to face three realities:

1. The best candidates already have good jobs and are not actively looking for a job – you will have to find them, recruit and poach them from their current employer.

There will be an increased investment of time and money required to find and recruit.

. You must have **your version** of a *'Start with Us – Stay with Us'* plan; a path of opportunity forward and upward inside your business, and / or…if necessary; after their 2–5-year contribution to your business, you then provide a path of leaving and moving to a bigger company or entrepreneurial venture…maybe even with your backing.

You are **competing to get employees worth having**, which requires…a crafted opportunity that you can market and sell, a method of presenting your company and opportunity in an unorthodox, attention-getting way, e.g. Taco Bell's hiring party, and personal interaction, not just on-line.

Mired In Meetings?

'Call To Order'

A Harvard Business Review survey indicated Harvard Business Review survey indicated that 65% of business executives stated that meetings keep them from completing their work.

71% stated the meetings at their companies are unproductive and inefficient. 64% stated that meetings come at the cost of a lack of meaningful thinking. 62% indicated that their meetings failed to bring their team closer.

Now, for the mystery, with such high agreement that the majority of meetings are a waste of time, why do they keep happening and everyone still takes part? **Why no rebellion?**

I know someone who became the number one salesperson at a large insurance brokerage. He was asked to speak at one of the daily morning sales meetings, to explain to all how he was outselling.

His secret…he revealed that he scheduled breakfast sales appointments at the same time as the company's daily morning sales meetings, so he didn't have to attend the meetings. He was subsequently terminated.

Research indicates that **meetings inside companies have** *increased in length **plus** frequency,* almost every year for the last 50 years!

Notwithstanding the improvements in technology, communication tools, media, etc., business managers are spending an average of 23 hours a week using these tools, compared to 10 hours a week in the 1980's.

Some want to make the point that this is a price to pay that's worth it, to get the collaboration, creativity and team 'buy-in', **despite a lack of evidence to support that idea**.

Finally, this part of management intersects with marketing, at the point of accountability. Really?? Is there financial proof that this belief will move the needle?

I not only disagree, I know better, and not only from experience but from my study and product development of my **P.A.T.** meeting system.

Core Values on Your Customers

The starting point for truly great customer service isn't thrilling, *but crucial*; your core values, your mission statement, whatever is at the heart of your business must place a massive emphasis on your customer.

If you don't, it will be apparent daily, and your team members *won't believe you when you say that customer service is crucial* and will be exhibited in terms of the quality of service, they give your customers.

In all the businesses I owned, I didn't read my company value statement often, but it was the basis of how we rolled. Our values were simple:

✓ **Take care of our team members**
✓ **Take care of our customers**
✓ **Always do what is right**

You'll notice that taking care of our team members is before taking care of our customers, but please appreciate that these core values aren't numbered, but bulletined, e.g. none is more important than another, but in this order for a reason.

I believed that if we took care of team members, they would take great care of our customers.

Please understand, when I said 'take care of team members', I didn't mean welfare or baby-sitting. I meant **'providing team members with the means to help them achieve their career and personal goals!**

In some cases that means helping them find another job. I have helped key employees to further their careers with such companies as Nike, Microsoft and Wells Fargo.

How do your core values affect your bottom line?

The *'Ethics Resource Center'* did an analysis of the Dow Jones for a period of 30 years. At the time they found that if you invested $30K in the Dow for 30 years, you would have a return of $134K.

Next, they studied 21 companies on the Dow that had a **written** and **published** value statement that specified that their company's purpose and function was to serve the public with *high ethical standards*.

Had you invested that same $30K with those 21 companies with high ethical standards, your return would have exceeded $1,000,000.00.

What do you do now? Define your core values in **writing, publish** it, **install** with your team members and **tell your customers!**

Leadership Plan

I am confident this book is inspirational. However, inspiration without a decision and a decision without execution is futile. That's what 97% do. They get what they have always gotten, because they continue to do what they have always not done.

Whenever you begin to shirk, re-read this book. Whenever you need to rekindle your inspiration, re-read this book. Every time you re-read this book, you will sustain your 'stick-to-itiveness' and determination to profitable success.

Look back on your life five years ago, and ask yourself…

'Do I want to be in the same place five years from now?'

Tired of so-called experts and sales trainers telling you how to run your business when they've never done it themselves?

Ron Hequet –

Driven by Results, Guided by Experience

This program is NOT for you if...

- You'd rather conform to what most business managers do!
- You don't want to rise above the average income of most business owners in your industry!
- You tend to be negative, whine, complain or blame outside circumstances for results.
- You believe this program would be an **expense** instead of an **investment!**

The VIP 3 % 'Winners Circle'™...find out if it's right for you by scheduling your free introductory assessment – go NOW to...

www.RonHequet/Mentor-Programs.com

or

www.ProfitandCashflowMarketing.com

ADMISSION IS LIMITED: If there is no program availability at time of enrollment, you will be placed on the aged waiting list.

A client told me, **"I don't have any money."** I responded with, **"I know you don't have any money,** *that's why I am here.* **"**
– Ron Hequet

Additional Resources

PROFIT AND CASH FLOW MARKETING...FAST©

10 WAYS TO OUTTHINK...OUT MARKET...OUTSELL YOUR COMPETITION...IN ANY ECONOMY!

BOOK

**To invest in additional resources...go to:
www.RonHequet.com**

Additional Resources

THE PROFIT GROWTH CALCULATOR™

HOW I FIND 10K IN ANY BUSINESS IN 45 MINUTES

BOOK

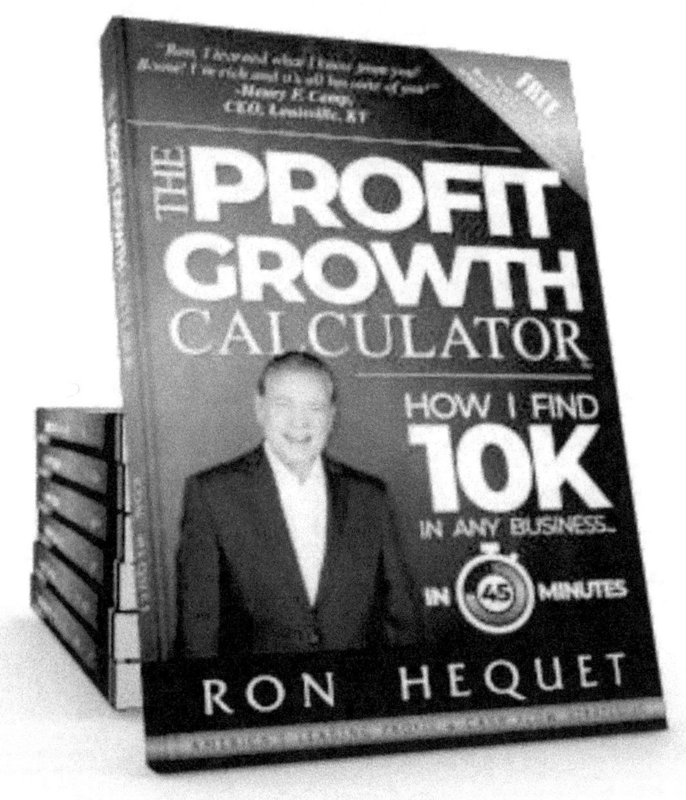

To invest in additional resources...go to:
www.RonHequet.com